Appropriating the Discourse of Social Justice in Teacher Education

Appropriating the Discourse of Social Justice in Teacher Education

Marta P. Baltodano

ROWMAN & LITTLEFIELD
Lanham • Boulder • New York • London

Published by Rowman & Littlefield
A wholly owned subsidary of The Rowman & Littlefield Publishing Group, Inc.
4501 Forbes Boulevard, Suite 200, Lanham, Maryland 20706
www.rowman.com

Unit A, Whitacre Mews, 26-34 Stannary Street, London SE11 4AB

British Library Cataloguing in Publication Information Available

Library of Congress Cataloging-in-Publication Data

Baltodano, Marta.
Appropriating the discourse of social justice in teacher education / Marta P. Baltodano.
pages cm
Summary: "Appropriating the Discourse of Social Justice in Teacher Education is a testimony to that
kind of authentic reform. It documents the transformational efforts of a teacher education program
that infused the preparation of its teachers with a vision of education as a public good. This book
validates the claim that the process of reproduction of social inequalities in teacher education is not a
perfect, static process, but on the contrary, the real 'seeds of transformation' within teacher education
departments are abundant" —Provided by publisher.
Includes bibliographical references
ISBN 978-1-60709-744-0 (hardback) — ISBN 978-1-60709-745-7 (paper) — ISBN 978-1-60709-
746-4 (electronic)
1. Teachers—Training of—Social aspects.—United States. 2. Social justice—Study and teaching—
United States. I. Title.
LB1715.B34 2015
371.102—dc23
2014046912

∞™ The paper used in this publication meets the minimum requirements of American
National Standard for Information Sciences Permanence of Paper for Printed Library
Materials, ANSI/NISO Z39.48-1992.

Printed in the United States of America

To Albert and Emanuel whose unconditional love and support made this book possible.

To the faculty, supervisors, and student-teachers at Laurel Canyon University whose journey brings us hope about the transformation of teacher education.

Contents

Foreword

Words, Words, Words: Discourse Theft in the Twenty-First Century

Shirley R. Steinberg

In frustration, Eliza Doolittle chortles a simplistic cantata regarding her annoyance with Henry Higgins: "Words, words, words, I'm so sick of words . . . I get words all day through, first from him, now from you" (lyrics by Alan Lerner, 1956). As a critical educator, I identify with Eliza's disgust at the useless nature of language in many situations. The more words I hear through educational discourse, the less they mean. With global words shooting 'round the world, it takes the proverbial nanosecond for a sender to blast the message into cyberspace and for the receiver to get it—in traditional media theory, this model of communication depends on a channel to contain the message. One would expect that in the short time the message is "channeled" that little would occur that could possible alter the message. As humans, however, we must always assume that the message could morph—indeed, it could be interpreted differently than intended by the original sender. What traditional media theory doesn't articulate is that instead of misinterpretation of the message, a hijacking could occur. In fact, with my cynical notion of educational discourse, I assert that hijacking is the norm rather than the occasional bleep.

Years ago, while teaching in New York City, City University of New York (CUNY) professors attended a meeting with erstwhile mayoral candidate/pundit/self-described liberal Mark Green. Green was discussing funding for universities and specific grants for educators. In a list of do's and don'ts for receiving these grants, Green told the audience that there were specific words and phrases to avoid. Noting that the political climate for New York followed the dominant flood of conservatism in education, Mark gave us the two major don'ts for grant applications: 1) do not mention democracy, and 2) do not use the phrase *social justice*.

Indeed, discourses have changed, but political intervention into the notion of fair and equitable education has not. In the twenty-first century a linguistic phenomenon has taken place. Instead of fearing words and phrases such as *social justice, democracy, marginalization, diversity,* and *disenfranchisement,* conservatives have hijacked and redefined the words. Like advertising think tanks, the right wing has targeted a market of ignorant and naive political consumers and used the language of the left to woo, and indeed, convert populations. And it has worked. Incanting phrases that include *peace, bipartisanship,* and *democratic citizens,* the political right has managed to take control of the discourse that began to combat the inequities of conservative policies.

In 1983, President Reagan endorsed the creation of the National Commission on Excellence in Education, consisting of politicians from both American political groups. The commission published *A Nation at Risk,* a document seeding the notion that American schools were failing and the fault was in the teachers, the curriculum, and the schools. This document led to the demand for "back to basics" educational initiatives that eventually led to Two Thousand Points of Light (Bush the Elder), No Child Left Behind (Bush the Younger), and Race to the Top (Obama). The titles of each document or movement themselves sold conservative goods to gullible public school parents and voters who, in all honesty, just wanted their kids to succeed. *A Nation at Risk* immediately set the stage for the fearmongering that has controlled American (also Canadian, British, Australian, New Zealand, and Northern Europe) educational dialogues for almost thirty years. Titling the document did not interrogate the question, if indeed, the nation was at risk: it reinforced a tenet that was never questioned. The nation was at risk, and the commission, with Christofundamentalist, compulsive gambler William Bennett at the helm, was there to save us. Schools were inundated with workshops and texts that demanded a return to basic phonics, the three R's, and the elimination of the curriculum of frills ushered in by the educational left of the 1960s and 1970s; art, drama, creative writing, music, and physical education classes began to become minimized, and mathematics, science, and reading (not literature) were declared the salvation of education. Americans were told that they were not number one in the competition to be the best-educated country in the world . . . and as we know, Americans must be number one.

After Reagan, Bennett, and the boys began the back-to-basics tornado, Daddy Bush followed up by declarations that would usher in the new millennium. Part of his plan was to ensure that every child would know how to read by the year 2000. We all know how that ended. Clinton did little to raise the value of American schooling, and he avoided discussions involving social justice . . . it was just too radical for his taste. When Boy Bush entered the fray, he was determined to question if "all our children is learning." In order to boost the test scores of Texas schoolchildren, the one-term Governor Bush (along with Rod Paige) had raised scores in standardized testing by leaps and bounds. It only took making sure that special education and immigrant children's scores were not counted—Houston was particularly affected, and the city's score change became known as The Houston Miracle. In a *60 Minutes* exposé, the miracle was found to be fraudulent as teachers had not only falsified test results but had been given financial bonuses to do so. One cannot miss the irony in light of Henry Giroux's and Peter McLaren's 1988 observation that teachers, indeed, were pawns of the ruling class. The Texas debacles brought their words to a new level. President Bush Jr. used his personal familial relationship with a Texas family, the McGraws, to endorse McGraw-Hill's introduction to new texts based on No Child Left Behind (NCLB). Splashing out expensive brochures and lesson plans, the new act demanded that literacy could be increased if earlier curricula such as whole language was replaced by a phonics-based program. NCLB never identified which children were being left behind, but using the discourse of social concern, it was hard to publicly argue against the notion. How exactly could one suggest that we should leave some children behind? Schools that did not rely on government grants were able to opt out of the NCLB demands, and teachers in disenfranchised neighborhoods were pressed into the factory mode of assembly-line curriculum involving teaching to the test. Monies were at stake—if scores were not raised, schools lost money.

Paige, Bush Jr.'s Secretary of Education, rose from making miracles in Houston to governing the educational system of the United States for over five years. The author of a reported sixty-page dissertation on the response time of football linesmen, the leader of American teachers and students brought a new low to incompetence. Glossy brochures on teacher preparation became the clarion cry to make sure all children progressed. Trotting in politically right-wing advisors, the Department of Education did little more than suppress teacher incentive and educational creativity and increase teacher burnout, student dropouts, and the cancellation of school programs and funding. Private enterprises sprouted up—Success for All, Voyager, Channel One, AUSSIE—for-profit groups whose messianic messages promised to save the hoards of children at risk. Teachers were subject to constant redevelopment programs, all aimed at making it better.

During the reign of Bush Jr., a linguistic change in the rhetoric of the right echoed through the country. Those pundits and politicos who had criticized liberal initiatives such as diversity, multiculturalism, and creativity began to use the language originally attributed to the left. Instead of critiquing progressive education, the right began to declare its own agenda of progressivism. In the sciences, creationism became intelligent design; teacher payoffs became merit increases; Republican voters became the disenfranchised; and white, middle-class students became the marginalized, forgotten students.

Like many liberal and progressive initiatives, social justice was stolen by a right-wing thief in the night. Citizens began to interpret messages through channels without understanding that the messages themselves had been stolen. Americans, untrained in critical deconstruction or a sense of discourse discernment, have largely been fed a decade of linguistic tripe that masks itself as responsible pedagogy dedicated to equity and success. Legitimated by accountability groups, most notably the National Council for Accreditation of Teacher Education (NCATE), teachers and administrators have become hostages to profit-generating, private-corporate examination of public schools and curriculum.

The practice of blame ramped up in the new millennium, creating mass parental hysteria, and media punditry entered the channels of communication and authored message interference. In 2010, *Waiting for Superman* was released, supported by the big kahunas, Oprah and Bill Gates. The film waged a war against labor-organized teachers, and it made a compelling case for privatized charter schools. Earlier in the decade, Educational Management Organizations (EMOs) sprang up, for-profit businessmen and women who promised to come into troubled schools and manage them. Modeled from groups like the Edison Project, these EMOs were staffed by corporate groups, banks, and dot-coms, and they paraded in troops of business managers (none of whom had pedagogical backgrounds) who promised to put educational ships in shape. Citizens were outraged at the notion that American teachers had been forming unions whose only goals were to get large pay increases, more vacation time, to ignore parents, and who refused to teach to the standards implemented by NCLB and Race to the Top. By focusing on teaching unions, viewers were convinced that all American states were controlled by renegade teaching unions and that the state of American education was in danger . . . the solution: to privatize schools and end centralized administration and the involvement of big government in public schools.

In a recent meeting with the then-governor of New York's right-hand education man, Joe Frey, I was told about the new curriculum being designed for alternative teaching education. *Alternative* was the word being used to describe a process in which an aspiring teacher would enter a one-year, fully funded program after completing a BA in any field but education. The candidate would have a full year of coursework and field teaching and receive a New York State teaching certificate while holding a full-time teaching position as field experience. I was told that the program was being designed by Pearson and would be ready within the year. Pearson? Pearson? After years of teaching in New York State, I couldn't recall a professor or New York State education employee of that name. I stopped Frey and asked who Pearson was . . . was he the curriculum developer, a professor, a school administrator? Frey looked at me curiously. Pearson was "Pearson Publishing, they are designing the entire new curriculum for both elementary and regents education." Choking on my thoughts, I responded, "Ah, so who is working with Pearson? I know most of the people in the state who would be on the task force, I am just curious to see who Pearson is working with." Frey smiled, "None of your people. Pearson knows what they are doing. I am sure that after the curriculum is finished, they will run it by some of you." Gulp.

Critical pedagogy creates a discourse that names that which is being done, heard, and initiated—it names sources of power and economic gain at the expense of students and schools. Instead of hiding behind neoliberal attempts to keep all political sides content, those engaged in critical pedagogical readings of the world identify how power works and controls within the educational environment. Marta Baltodano does exactly this in *Appropriating the Discourse of Social Justice in Teacher Education*. Engaging in an ethnographic study, Marta contends that teacher education can change, and can be transformative. This book is a rich discussion that presents a research study with thick description and informed interpretation, and that takes back the linguistic stolen goods from the right. Naming her own positionality as a Latina educator and scholar, she presents an authentic portrait of educational malaise in North American schools.

Using a Bourdieusian notion of how capital is reproduced, Marta examines through a critical ethnographic lens ways in which a school attempts to create an authentic approach to incorporating social justice. Understanding that just declaring that social justice is the goal and heart of a school is not the same as facilitating its influence. Underpinning this work is a tightly woven cloth of critical educational theory, laying out a new sociology of education. Marta exemplifies a rigorous research tradition as she leads the theoretical discussion into the notions of hegemony and social reproduction, and enters into a critical pedagogical framework of hope with the commitment to transformative practices and conscientização. Examining ideology and reminding the reader that transformative cultural work is based on reading the political world and identifying how power works, the book leads us to an examination of a teacher education program and the surrounding community.

This book is one of a very few critical ethnographic works that uses and carries out the intellectual exercises of theoretical grounding, political and ideological readings, the ethnographical read, a phenomenological analysis, and a critical hermeneutic discussion of *what went wrong*. The honest and thickly researched book is a cultural work of social justice, and it is a welcome addition to our needs, as critical intellectual educators historicize, politicize, and criticize the work we are doing. I found this book powerful and believe it will stand a test of time in its ability to inform those engaged in the pursuit and facilitation of empowering, transformative, critical pedagogy. Marta's work gives us hope within the context of those *words, words, words.*

Shirley R. Steinberg is the cofounder and director of The Paulo and Nita Freire International Project for Critical Pedagogy. She has recently been appointed as the Werklund Foundation Chair of Youth Leadership at the University of Calgary and has been research professor at the University of Barcelona. She is the author and editor of many books in critical pedagogy, urban and youth culture, and cultural studies. Her most recent books include: *Kinderculture: The Corporate Construction of Childhood* (2011); *Teaching Against Islamophobia* (2010); *19 Urban Questions: Teaching in the City* (2010); *Christotainment: Selling Jesus through Popular Culture* (2009); *Diversity and Multiculturalism: A Reader* (2009); *Media Literacy: A Reader* (2007); and the award-winning *Contemporary Youth Culture.* She is also the founding editor of *Taboo: The Journal of Culture and Education* and the managing editor of *The International Journal of Critical Pedagogy.*

Introduction

The cultural revolution of the 1960s represented one of the most significant movements in American history. Schools and universities were centers of dissent, intellectual diversity, civic engagement, and political activism. The civil rights movement and the antiwar protests had particular meaning because of the robust participation of students, teachers, and university faculty in the civic struggle. There was an interruption to the traditional vision of universities as elitist and isolated repositories of intellectual life.

American intelligentsia took to the streets and refused to play the role of apologists of the status quo. That countercultural movement marked an era in which American universities became the expression of public democratic life. Those were the 1960s, at the pinnacle of the liberal state, and during America's last attempt to create a humanist capitalism.

Twenty years later, during the 1980s, the Reagan administration dismantled the welfare state and most of the social reforms implemented in the previous years through a series of economic policies known as Reaganomics. That decade marked a conservative period characterized by the belief that the social reforms of the past decades had failed and that years of protectionism and civil rights activism had hurt the economy.

As at any other time of economic transition and political turmoil, schools, which traditionally play a pivotal role adjusting societal discourse, became scapegoats and were blamed for the inequalities created by the unregulated market. Public education was accused of being ineffective and mediocre. Schools and teachers were criticized and urged to change the school curriculum to improve students' test scores. The government and business groups instilled fear in the public that the decline of American economic power was imminent if schools were not fixed. Schools, teachers, and their unions were portrayed as institutions that were compromising the success of the American economy.

Public opinion was deeply influenced by the publication of a series of reports on the state of public education. Among them were *A Nation at Risk: The Imperative for Educational Reform* (1983); *A Nation Prepared: Teachers for the 21st Century* (1986); *Tomorrow's Teachers* (1986); *Time for Results: The Governors' 1991 Report on Education*; and *Goals 2000*. These reports, particularly *A Nation at Risk*, blamed schools for what appeared to be the failure of the American educational system to produce competitive workers for the new economy. Americans began losing confidence in the revered institution of public schooling, and they became convinced that something was wrong with public education.

In 1990, the U.S. Secretary of Energy, Admiral James Watkins, commissioned the Sandia National Laboratories to conduct a study to support President George H. W. Bush's policies to reform public schools (Tanner, 1993, p. 290). The Department of Energy was interested in confirming that American education was deteriorating in order to give priority to sciences and mathematics education. However, in a surprising twist, the three researchers from the Sandia National Laboratories concluded that U.S. education was not declining, and that in fact American students were performing better than previous years according to data from federal and national agencies.

The Sandia report was immediately censured and withheld, though many years later it was published with substantial revisions and never widely disseminated. The Sandia Report brought back some sense of decency to the discussion after its findings invalidated the claim that American education was dramatically declining. What became clear is that the hysterical attacks against public education were just part of a manufactured crisis (Berliner & Biddle, 1995; Gabbard, 1999) to move from decades of emphasis on access to education—desegregation, special education—to a focus on accountability and standardization (Graham, 2003).

The war on public education initiated in the 1980s continued at the onset of the new century with the approval of the No Child Left Behind Act (NCLB). This legislation that represented the culmination of years of conservative educational policies took away the tradition of local control of schools and raised the status of the standardization movement to the level of a federal policy, enforcing at once the contested tenet that students' test scores are the end product and ultimate goal of public education (Amrein & Berliner, 2003; McLaren & Baltodano, 2005; Symcox, 2009).

The decision to penalize and reward teachers and schools based on publicized students' test scores caused a great deal of concern among parents, teachers, and administrators. The pressure was so intense that cheating scandals spread nationwide.[1] Because test scores reflect a myriad of influences, including the students' family income, language proficiency, and special education status, schools in working-class communities of color failed year after year. As a result, these schools were shut down, reconstituted, and offered "for sale" because they could not meet NCLB's intended academic proficiencies.

This trend to privatize "failing" public schools and convert them into charter schools managed by nonprofit charter management organizations (CMOs) or for-profit businesses has been the signature approach of the Obama administration. The appointment of Arne Duncan, the former CEO of the Chicago public schools, as Obama's secretary of education and the one responsible for closing more than seventy public schools during his tenure, clearly conveyed that this presidency has not been any different from the previous ones regarding educational policies.

One of Obama's first initiatives, the Race to the Top competition, which follows in the footsteps of No Child Left Behind, was funded to promote a contest among the states about who could demonstrate greater school achievement, as demonstrated by test scores, adoption of standards, expansion of charter schools, implementation of test scores–driven teacher evaluations, and the reconstitution of failing schools (Ravitch, 2013). The five-billion-dollar allocation to the Race to the Top competition reflects the common goals of the Obama government and the new wave of corporate educational reformers who relentlessly continue the attacks against public education.

For teacher preparation programs, the situation has become more problematic since the publication of the several reports attacking teachers and the universities that prepare them. One of the most intense targets has been traditional teacher preparation programs that have a student-teaching component and a coaching model to prepare and induct preservice teachers. Teach for America and venture philanthropists seeking to privatize public education have strongly criticized this traditional teacher education model because they deem it lengthy, expensive, and unnecessary.

Duncan has spent most of his tenure encouraging the creation of alternative certification models and attacking schools of education, in spite of the fact that abundant research links student achievement to teacher preparation that includes an extended residency (Cochran-Smith & Fries, 2001; Darling-Hammond, 2000, 2001; Weiner, 2007; Zeichner, 2006). Alternative routes to teacher certification have proliferated as a result of the constant subsidy and strategic donations given by venture philanthropies (Kumashiro, 2010; Ravitch, 2013; Saltman, 2009; Scott, 2009).

Universities are also creating alternative teacher certification programs to remain competitive in the aggressive educational market. Schools of education, as the "cash cows" of most universities, are pressured to increase student enrollment to compete with all the purveyors of public and private education, which includes online universities, for-profit colleges, and private educational enterprises. The pressure to increase student enrollment and make teacher education departments more marketable has also increased the demands for national accreditation.

The National Council for Accreditation of Teacher Education (NCATE) played a powerful role in 1977 when it required the inclusion of multicultural education in teacher education to address the issues advanced by the civil rights movement. However, since the publications of the reports attacking teacher education in the early 1980s, NCATE became a regulator of the educational market and led the reform efforts to align teacher preparation to NCLB, Race to the Top, and several corporate-sponsored initiatives.

Thus, in 2000, NCATE revamped its accreditation requirements and consolidated its twenty benchmarks into six new revised standards. These benchmarks were again slightly revised in 2008 (see table 0.1). From the six standards, it was standard four on Diversity that was the one that caught people's imagination, as it appeared to follow the advocacy tradition that NCATE exhibited in 1977 when it advocated for the inclusion of multiculturalism.

Table 0.1.   NCATE and CAEP Accreditation Standards

	NCATE	CAEP
Standard 1	Candidate Knowledge, Skills, and Professional Dispositions	Content and Pedagogical Knowledge
Standard 2	Assessment System and Unit Evaluation	Clinical Partnerships and Practice
Standard 3	Field Experiences and Clinical Practice	Candidate Quality, Recruitment, and Selectivity
Standard 4	Diversity	Program Impact
Standard 5	Faculty Qualifications, Performance, and Development	Provider Quality Assurance and Continuous Improvement
Standard 6	Unit Governance and Resources	

Yet in the new century, within the context of the attacks against teacher education and with the increasing corporatization of schools of education, this standard was misused. Colleges of education, in their attempt to conform to NCATE requirements, skillfully produced conceptual frameworks and mission statements portraying their teacher preparation programs as institutions devoted to social justice issues.

Schools and colleges of education changed their academic degrees or the name of their programs to include the term *social justice* with the intent of obtaining national accreditation and increasing their marketability (Weiner, 1993, 2007). Many of these teacher preparation programs used the diversity lexicon for recruitment purposes, but their pedagogical and administrative practices were still anchored on ethnocentric views of the world.

Nevertheless, NCATE's standard on Diversity and its association with the concept of social justice triggered an alarming response from conservative groups. As a result, in 2007, NCATE withdrew the term *social justice* from its accreditation training documents to respond to concerns that the council was emphasizing too much diversity.

This is how NCATE framed this decision:

> NCATE has never required a "social justice" disposition; NCATE expects institutions to select professional dispositions they would like to see in the teachers they prepare. The term "social justice," though well understood by NCATE's institutions, was widely and wildly misinterpreted by commentators not familiar with the workings of NCATE. NCATE has never had a "social justice" standard and thus did not enforce such a standard. (http://www.ncate.org)

If there was any hope that NCATE would reaffirm its original role of advocating for the inclusion of social justice, diversity, and equity, as it did in 1977, this statement leaves no doubts about NCATE's political orientation.

In 2013, after several years of negotiation, NCATE merged with the Teacher Education Accreditation Council (TEAC) to form the Council for the Accreditation of Educator Preparation (CAEP), which will begin accrediting teacher preparation programs in 2016. This merge, which was funded by the Broad Foundation and other venture philanthropies and was urged by the government and business groups, represents several years of planning to produce a new organization and a new set of standards to substantially transform the field of teacher education.

One of the most important changes that the new CAEP standards bring to the accreditation process is the emphasis on "Program Impact" (standard 4) (see table 0.1). CAEP will grant national accreditation to teacher preparation programs that demonstrate with hard data that their teachers are improving the test scores of the students in the schools where they teach. This hard data includes the highly controversial value-added measures supported by the Gates Foundation (Measures of Effective Teacher [MET] Project).

Customer satisfaction is also an important component of this standard, as "providers" (teacher preparation programs) need to present data about their teachers' employment milestones, such as promotion, retention, and evaluation of their employers. This information needs to be included in the "providers'" annual report to CAEP as part of its constant monitoring of accredited institutions (standard 5: Provider Quality Assurance and Continuous Improvement) (see table 0.1). The report should contain the following data:

Impact on P–12 learning and development; indicators of teaching effec-
tiveness; results of employer surveys, including retention and employment milestones; results of completer surveys; graduation rates; ability
of completers to meet licensing (certification) and any additional state
requirements; ability of completers to be hired in education positions
for which they were prepared; and student loan default rates and other
consumer information. (CAEP accreditation standards, 2013, p. 16)

In addition, the Board of Directors of CAEP has established a new
"'gold standard' level of accreditation reserved for only the best programs" (Sawchuk, 2013, p. 8), which follows into the footsteps of the
questionable group the National Council on Teacher Quality (NCTQ).
This newer organization, which was funded by conservative groups and
venture philanthropies, released a "public shaming"[2] report in 2013, con-
cluding that from the 1,200 teacher education institutions in the United
States, only four made the "Dean's List" (Bullough Jr., 2014, p. 185).

The Council warned consumers, "It is not just conceivable, but likely,
that many aspiring teachers and school districts will not be able to locate
a highly-rated program anywhere near them" (NCTQ, 2013, p. 57). This
group released a newer report in 2014 in a more conciliatory tone but
arriving at the same results. NCTQ has been widely criticized for the lack
of methodology and the inconsistencies of its findings.

Another variation in the new CAEP standards in addition to "Program Impact" is the issue of "Diversity." NCATE's standard 4 on "Diversity" was eliminated from the newer accreditation criteria and replaced
with CAEP standard 3 on "Candidate Quality, Recruitment, and Selectivity" (see table 0.1). This new benchmark calls for recruitment of "high
quality candidates from a broad range of backgrounds and diverse populations," while setting rigid admission benchmarks that surpass previous
admittances into teacher education.

This standard foresees that by the year 2018 to 2019 teacher education
programs will admit only those students who have a 3.0 GPA and, as a
group, these students will rank in the top third of the GRE, ACT, or SAT
tests.

As it happened in the past with NCATE's standard 4 on Diversity, the
newer CAEP standard on Candidate Quality, Recruitment, and Selectivity has been artfully crafted to provide the impression that the new national accrediting body of teacher preparation is really concerned about
creating a diverse teaching force. Nothing seems further away from the
truth when the excellence disclaimer limits the scope of the diverse population that could be recruited into teaching.

The juxtaposition of diversity and excellence has been part of the platform of Teach for America and other corporate educational reformers for
many years. And nothing would be wrong if this equation did not disre-
gard and ignore the way minority populations have been undereducated
and excluded from having access to quality education in this country.

There is already a concern about the implications of such a standard in the efforts of colleges of education to recruit diverse teachers. Stillman College president Ernest McNealey said on behalf of a group of deans of Historically Black Colleges,

> There will be fewer teachers with credentials from American colleges and universities; there will be an adverse impact on diversity in the teaching force, including gender, social class and race; and there will be a discriminatory stratification of institutions offering accredited teacher preparation programs based on historical advantages having little to do with preparing high performing teachers. (Hawkins, 2013, p. 15)

As NCATE's standard 4 on Diversity, CAEP's standard 3 on Candidate Quality, Recruitment, and Selectivity represents another distortion and appropriation of the concept of diversity and social justice. Through national accreditation, a liberal approach to diversity is institutionalized in teacher education. From that perspective, there is lip service to the issue of cultural difference, and there is a strong reliance on a policy of colored bodies and a make-feel-good ideology about cultural pluralism.

However, there is a refusal to engage with issues of power and oppression or to critically examine the structural and economic causes of poverty, racism, exploitation, violence, discrimination, and other forms of hegemony. This unwillingness to address issues of privilege and domination is masked under the discourse of excellence that is paraded as intrinsically linked to higher test scores in students and their teachers.

The inclusion of sanitized notions of diversity in the criteria for the national accreditation of teacher preparation programs is another accountability scheme (McLaren, 2002). Accountability schemes, along with *quality control* of teaching, are evidence of the growing business agenda of accrediting institutions and colleges of education. In this context, "diversity becomes just another commodity for students to consume and for programs to produce. Through national accreditation, successful commodification of diversity is rewarded by the marketable status symbol of accreditation" (Baltodano & Clemons, 2005). As a result, there are strong movements of reforms in teacher education. The most common ones are intended to adjust teacher preparation to the standardization demands of NCLB, Race to the Top, and CAEP to make teacher education more *accountable.*

These reforms carried out in the name of excellence, accountability, diversity, and inclusion constitute subliminal efforts to appropriate the possibilities for real transformation in teacher education. However, in spite of the pervasive rhetoric to identify diversity and social justice with the accountability and standardization movement, there are endeavors to create transformations in teacher preparation that are authentic.

These deliberate changes seek to counteract the neoliberal vision of school reform and strive to reclaim the original goals of public education represented in a vision of rigorous content knowledge, democratic schooling, and social justice (Giroux, 2008; Novak, 1994). This book is a testimony to that kind of authentic reform. It documents the transformational efforts of a teacher education program that infuses the preparation of its teachers with a vision of education as a public good.

These changes were inspired in the seminal work of philosophers of education, educational activists, and critical theorists who envisioned teacher education and public schools as democratic spheres where teachers and students engage in the connections between education and freedom (Dewey, 1916; Du Bois, 1935; Freire, 1970; Greene, 1982; Horton, 1998).

This book describes the journey led by Samantha, the director of the teacher education program, and the other professors and students who drove the changes to radically transform the teacher preparation program at Laurel Canyon University.[3] However, this story did not have a happy conclusion. After several years of leading the transformational efforts, Samantha, a junior faculty, and Teresa, a senior professor, were pushed out of their administrative and teaching positions and had to leave the university.

In spite of the strong support of students and faculty, these professors overlooked the powerful conservative forces that were managing the College of Education and the larger university. The transformation of their teacher education program could not be afforded by the university administration because it was jeopardizing its most profitable academic program and the one that was subsidizing the doctoral degrees. These professors were ill prepared to deal with the corporatization of higher education and the demands to align teacher education to the needs of the market.

Nevertheless, this book validates the claim presented by Beyer and Zeichner (1987) that the process of reproduction of social inequalities in teacher education is not a perfect, static process, but on the contrary, the real "seeds of transformation" within teacher education departments are abundant. In fact, what is needed is a set of strategies for those committed to reclaim teacher preparation programs as democratic spaces (Giroux & McLaren, 1988). This book provides such recommendations.

NOTES

1. See, for example, Haney, 2000, "The Myth of the Texas Miracle in Education," and Jarvie, 2014, "School Cheating Trial Set to Open." The latter article documents the current Atlanta trial in which twelve Black teachers and administrators were accused of falsely boosting students' test scores and were prosecuted under Georgia's Racketeer Influenced and Corrupt Organizations statute.

2. This is how Sharon Robinson (2014), president of the American Association of Colleges for Teacher Education (AACTE), called the NCTQ reports.

3. The names of professors, students, university, and city mentioned in this book are fictitious to protect the identity of the participants.

ONE

Conducting Ethnography in Teacher Education

I began my incursion as a researcher of teacher education when I conducted a comparative critical ethnography of two teacher preparation programs. The first part of the ethnographic study, "Learning to Teach: Reproducing a Pedagogy of Oppression" was informed by theories of social and cultural reproduction, and it aimed to understand how society reproduces the beliefs of the dominant groups through the main actors of the schooling process, teachers.

The first part of the study documented the culture of teacher education in a state university and the process through which students internalize the values of the dominant society in university classrooms while learning to become teachers. An analysis of the diverse components of that particular teacher preparation program shed a light on how the dominant society's values illuminated the new teachers' pedagogical practices responsible for the efficient reproduction of social inequalities.

That study revealed that the process of social reproduction does not initiate at schools, but rather at teacher training programs where teachers learn the values of the dominant society and transmit them under the role of caretakers (Giroux & McLaren, 1988). However, that reseach also uncovered that the reproduction of the hegemonic discourse in schools is not a perfect or static process, but rather a dialectical, contradictory, and contested terrain, manifested in the efforts of some progressive students and faculty who resisted the alienation process.

Those findings suggested that there were real "seeds of transformation" (Beyer & Zeichner, 1987) in teacher preparation manifested in continuous, but unorganized, counterhegemonic efforts to transform the education of teachers. This book is a followup to those findings. It is based on the second part of the ethnographic research study that was conducted at a private university in California.

Grounded on a theory of agency and resistance, *Appropriating the Discourse of Social Justice in Teacher Education* documents the journey of a group of faculty and students who, led by a new director of a teacher preparation program, sought to transform a traditional, liberal, multicultural teacher education program into an authentic social justice–oriented department (Liston & Zeichner, 1987; Novak, 1994).

This book describes the journey, successes, obstacles, and the outcome of that transformational experience. It portrays the story of Samantha, the director of the teacher education program, the students, and the other professors who helped carry out the changes at the college of education.

This ethnography study suggests that in spite of the strict control of state agencies and public policy organizations, teacher preparation programs can change and be reclaimed as cultural sites to transform the teaching profession and schools. It also suggests that there are viable initiatives that can create space in teacher education for the education of strong teachers who visualize their work and their profession as part of a larger advocacy movement for social justice (Adams, Bell & Griffin, 2007; Ayers, Hunt & Quinn, 1998; Haberman, 1988, 1995).

However, the journey described in this book did not have a successful conclusion. Ideals, values, knowledge, hard work, and motivation were not enough. In spite of the strong support of the students and faculty, the leaders of the program overlooked the powerful conservative forces that were managing the college of education and the larger university. The transformation of the teacher education program could not be afforded by the university administration. It could jeopardize its most profitable academic program—its *cash cow*—and the one that was subsidizing the other academic degrees.

Educators committed to social justice need to be aware that under the increasing corporatization of higher education, teacher education programs are expected to be more profitable than ever. There are larger societal and university forces that will prevent any possible change on the nature of these programs for fear of declining enrollment.

Critical educators need to be armed with a clear set of strategic goals, political agendas, strong alliances, and, more importantly, the unconditional support of the top university administrators if they are committed to contest the dominant culture of their teacher preparation programs.

Appropriating the Discourse of Social Justice in Teacher Education provides a much-needed inside and in-depth examination of what it entails to authentically transform a social justice program. It helps teacher educators and administrators to deconstruct the distorted discourse of excellence and diversity sponsored by NCATE, CAEP, and other corporate educational reformers. It also provides a political economic analysis of the viability of radical transformations of teacher education, and it suggests that the success of such changes depends on a set of conditions.

This book offers recommendations to engage in a long-term and successful journey to educate teachers to foment a real participatory democracy in the classroom, and therefore in the larger society.

AN EMIC VIEWPOINT AND MY INSIDER ROLE

My work as a teacher educator at Laurel Canyon University was marked by ambivalent feelings of frustration and hope. The teacher education program prided itself on being one of the most culturally diverse programs in California. Its leaders argued that because more than 50 percent of its students were people of color they could technically apply for the same funding and privileges that Historically Black Colleges were receiving. However, minority students were confused by some of the discrepancies they were experiencing.

In spite of the strong rhetoric on multiculturalism, students of color felt invisible in a sea of privilege dominated by predominantly Caucasian and upper-middle-class classmates. They did not have any influence to alter the correlation of power at the university or department level, and their presence was just a manifestation of the policy of colored bodies that the university had developed.

In fact, the development office continued to organize photo shoots of students of color taken individually and as a group to be included in the university brochures. The students were very conscious that the discourse on multiculturalism was part of the university effort to become more marketable and to increase enrollment, particularly because it was located in one of the most diverse regions in California. They saw the publicized emphasis on cultural diversity as part of the corporatization process that was under way at Laurel Canyon University.

The implementation of the new multicultural teaching credential in California drove me to examine whether the department in which I was working was adequately preparing teachers to work with children who were culturally different from the predominantly white, heterosexual, and middle-class teaching force. I sought to investigate how genuine were the efforts of the university to diversify its students and the teaching force it was preparing, taking into account the experiences of the minority students in the department and in the larger university.

During my years as a faculty member at Laurel Canyon University, I worked under the direction of two different administrations. I became a participant observer in all my different roles to grasp the entire dimension of this teacher education culture—faculty in the teacher education department, member of search committees, supervisor, mentor, interviewer of candidates to the program, and researcher. The examination of the transformational journey of the teacher education program at Laurel Canyon University took place in two separate stages.

The first part was conducted in 1998, and it included an examination of brochures; university catalogs; policy description; list of courses; bilingual programs; syllabi; accreditation review documents; observations of meetings and courses; interviews of faculty, administrators, and advisors; and focus groups of student teachers.

The second part of the research inquiry began in the winter of 2000 and extended to 2010. I was encouraged by the political spaces created by the new director of teacher education, Samantha, a white, middle-class, senior teacher educator. I decided to document the changes that this assistant professor was carrying on while I continued my work as faculty and supervisor of student teachers.

The policies of this new administration brought me hope that teacher education was not a dead-end project, but rather, it could become a viable terrain to implement curricular, administrative, and ideological changes to authentically transform the education of teachers (Clandinin et al., 1993; Doyle, 1996).

I interviewed faculty, administrators, student teachers, and in-service teachers in order to understand some of the new developments of the program. I observed most of the core courses of the teacher preparation program. I videotaped thirty hours of classroom instruction and audiotaped twenty hours of curricular meetings and courses. I took copious field notes of classroom observations and administrative meetings, and I examined classroom visitation forms, which were the official vehicle of communication between the student teachers and their supervisors.

I also read the students' entrance essay, and I had access to their masters' theses. I reviewed the updated versions of course syllabi and participated in faculty professional development meetings where I had the opportunity of sharing the preliminary findings of this research—my understanding of the transformative process of the program. I was able to receive feedback from my fellow colleagues and supervisors as part of the dialogical data generation that is characteristic of critical ethnography (Anderson, 1989; Carspecken, 1996; Conquergood, 1991; Kincheloe & McLaren, 1994; Levinson, 1992; Quantz, 1992; Simon & Dippo, 1986).

I followed two different cohorts of student teachers: a group admitted in the winter of 2000 and a second group admitted in the summer of 2001. Seven in-service teachers decided to participate more deeply in this research, and they were interviewed individually in formal settings, in casual encounters, and in two focus study groups.

Two major research studies that I conducted concomitantly in the teacher education program have been incorporated in this study. One of them is the institutional research I carried out on the graduates of the teacher preparation program at Laurel Canyon University. I used in-depth questionnaires, surveys, casual letters, informal interviews, and observations to understand how this teacher preparation was addressing issues of teachers'attrition.

The other research is related to my participation as a member of the Joint Social Justice Commission of the Association of Teacher Educators (ATE) and the National Council for Social Sciences. The entire cohort of in-service teachers at Laurel Canyon responded to five open-ended questions regarding their views on social justice.

The findings of both studies have been incorporated into this ethnography, and they were also used to triangulate the data gathered through the other more traditional ethnographic methods used in this study—participant observation, classroom observations, focus groups, and interviews (Diesing, 1971). The final stages of the research took place in 2010 and included additional fieldwork in the form of newer follow-up interviews, analysis of documents, and additional coding and analysis.

CRITICAL ETHNOGRAPHY

One of the major features of this research is that I did not conduct a conventional ethnography (Spindler, 1988) to trace the transformation of a teacher education program, but I used a critical approach to ethnographic research more compatible with the principles of critical educational theory (Anderson, 1989; Carspecken and Apple, 1992; Conquergood, 1991; Kincheloe & McLaren, 1994; Levinson, Foley & Holland, 1996; Quantz, 1992; Simon & Dippo, 1986).

Critical ethnography does not differ substantially from traditional ethnography in the way the data are collected and the recommendations for a "good ethnography of schooling" are implemented regarding the contextualized, prolonged, and repetitive nature of the observations, but it differs in the way the information is interpreted, analyzed and presented" (Spindler, 1998, p. 104; Tesch, 1990). Attention to "trustworthiness" was an essential element of the critical research process manifested in the prolonged engagement, persistent observation, triangulation, peer debriefing, negative case analysis, members check, and audit trail of the research process (Lincoln & Guba, 1985).

This research study circularly moved from the five recognized stages of a critical ethnography: 1) compiling a primary record through collection of monological data; 2) preliminary reconstructive analysis; 3) dialogical data generation; 4) discovering system relations; and 5) using system relations to explain findings (Carspecken & Apple, 1992, p. 513; Carspecken, 1996).

However, one of the most important features of critical ethnography is that it recognizes that the process of knowledge production—the research—is absolutely conditioned by the researcher's values and identity and equally influenced by the power struggles encountered in the research site (Giroux, 2004; Harding, 1987; Lather, 1986; McLaren & Giarelli, 1995; Roman & Apple, 1990).

The journey to transform the teacher education program at Laurel Canyon University is presented in this book from the perspective of the "ethnographic eyes" (Frank, 1999) of a Latina, immigrant faculty who resisted the temptation to be "a fly on the wall" and resorted to encouraging institutional changes. Yet the stories are narrated from the native viewpoint. Samantha, Teresa, Vincent, Jose, and the voices of the other educators and teacher candidates articulate the culture of this teacher preparation program.

BOOK ORGANIZATION AND FORMAT

This book presents the findings of a critical ethnography of a teacher education program. It is an academic book, but it has been written using a storymaking model to describe the transformational journey of a teacher education process. It is character based, and it is an example of how anthropology of education has begun to explore the use of alternative literary genres to explore anthropological concerns. The ethnography is described through a narrative style that follows the convention of nonfiction books (Roman, 1992).

The purpose is to bring alive these stories collected through traditional academic research and present them in the classic story model with its corresponding emotional and political closure. With this new format, this book seeks to reach a wider audience and make the content of this research accessible, enjoyable, and inspiring for students, teacher educators, and the public in general.

Chapter 1 is the introduction to the book. Chapters 2 and 3 are devoted to an examination of the theoretical framework and the current literature on the ideology of teacher education. Chapter 4 is the description of the case study and the university where this research took place.

Chapter 5 presents the story of Samantha, the director of the program, told through the changes she carried out. Chapter 6 is the story of the state of misfortune: the unhappy ending of the story and the convoluted economic forces that precipitated this failure. Chapter 7 is an analysis of what went wrong in this transformational journey, and chapter 8 describes the recommendations and strategies to avoid the pitfalls of this experience.

TWO

Critical Educational Theory

THE NEW SOCIOLOGY OF EDUCATION

Progressive approaches in education have been influenced by Marxist theory, the work of the Frankfurt School, the New Sociology of Education, and the ideas of some of the most influential social thinkers of past centuries, among them W. E. B. Du Bois (1935), Antonio Gramsci (1971), Paulo Freire (1970), Louis Althusser (1969), and Michel Foucault (1980). Although the Frankfurt School does not present a unified philosophy, it developed one of the most coherent theoretical efforts to examine the nature of capitalist societies while rejecting orthodox Marxism. Significant to its project was a search for alternative social and political models.

The concern of the Frankfurt School about what makes possible the reproduction of oppressive social patterns and the viability of social transformation prompted the examination of some particular themes. Among them were a theory of capitalism, the structure of the state, the rise of the culture industry and mass culture, the role of the family structure and individual development, and the rise of positivism (Held, 1980).

Based on an extensive interdisciplinary analysis of these themes, the members of the Frankfurt School developed a theory of culture that made possible the examination of the role that schools play as agents of social and cultural reproduction. In addition, they provided a theoretical interpretation of how the dominant society reproduces its core values—including oppressive patterns of domination—and how resistance to that domination is subtly diverted into destructive oppositional outcomes (Giroux, 1983; Morrow & Torres, 1995).

The emergence of the New Sociology of Education under the auspices of the British School of Sociology was vital for the development of a theory of critical education. The work of structuralists such as Louis Al-

thusser (1969, 1971), Basil Bernstein (1971–1975, 1977), and other scholars
contributed to this defining moment in sociology, which was a reaction
against the old mainstream, rigid Parsonian approach to schooling, particularly, "against the scientific pretensions of objective knowledge in
both the educational and social science fields" (Wexler, 1987, p. 36).

As part of these concerns, two major streams of thought evolved from
the field of the New Sociology of Education. The first one examined the
forms of socialization within schools. Economists such as Samuel Bowles
and Herbert Gintis (1976) and culturalists such as Pierre Bourdieu and
Jean Claude Passeron (1977) examined how society reproduces itself and
perpetuates its ideological values through schools.

One of the most influential works in that field was *Schooling in Capitalist America*, authored by Bowles and Gintis (1976), who are considered the
fathers of reproduction theory. These authors challenged the liberal educational doctrine that visualizes schools as institutions that promote social mobility and equal opportunity. They argue that schools have been
designed to achieve the opposite: to reproduce social class hierarchy in
order to advance the capitalist economic model.

Bowles and Gintis contend that schools are antidemocratic, as they
mirror the unjust social relations of the workplace and they reward behaviors and skills that are necessary to succeed in a hierarchically divided labor force:

> [We argue] that the range of effective educational policy in the United
> States is severely limited by the role of schooling in the production of
> an adequate labor force in a hierarchically controlled and class-strat-
> ified production system. (p. 20)
>
> [. . .] We suggest that major aspects of educational organization
> replicate the relationships of dominance and subordinancy in the eco-
> nomic sphere. The correspondence between the social relation of
> schooling and work accounts for the ability of the educational system
> to produce an amenable and fragmented labor force. The experience of
> schooling, and not merely the content of formal learning, is central to
> this process. (Bowles & Gintis, 1976, p. 125)

Later on, Bourdieu and Passeron (1977) provided a wider interpretation of this theory in their book, *Reproduction in Education, Society and
Culture*. They argue that schools impose a view of the social order consis-
tent with the interest of the social elite, and they do so by validating the
cultural capital of the dominant society, which is indispensable for economic success and social mobility.

Bourdieu and Passeron assert that schools reinforce notions of inferiority in students who do not bring to the schools that "cultural capital,"
which Giroux (1983) defines as "the different sets of linguistic and cultural competencies that individuals inherit by way of the class-located
boundaries of their families" (p. 88).

These competencies are the social skills and dispositions that students learn in their privileged families, among them are character traits, mannerisms, and appreciation for high culture, "proper" dress codes, "proper" language, sophisticated consumption patterns, social contacts, and so forth. These series of competences are deemed vital to compete and succeed for positions of power in the larger society, as they represent the values and beliefs of the dominant society.

Bourdieu (1977) explains how the transmission of cultural capital operates in the educational system:

> [Schools] offer information and training which can be received and acquired only by subjects endowed with the system of predispositions that is the condition for the success of the transmission and of the inculcation of the culture. By doing away with giving explicitly to everyone what it implicitly demands of everyone, the educational system demands of everyone alike that they have what they do not give. This consists mainly of linguistic and cultural competence and that relationship of familiarity with culture, which can only be produced by family upbringing when it transmits the dominant culture. (Bourdieu, 1977, p. 494)

Bourdieu and Passeron also developed the concept of *symbolic violence* and *habitus* to characterize how the interests of the ruling groups are naturalized in the form of cultural norms and internalized as "subjective dispositions" through the schools.

> School today succeeds, with the ideology of natural "gifts" and innate "tastes," in legitimating the circular reproduction of social hierarchies and educational hierarchies. Thus, the most hidden and most specific function of the education system consists in hiding its objective function, that is, masking the objective truth of its relationship to the structure of class relation. (Bourdieu & Passeron, 1977, p. 208)

Another seminal contribution to the development of reproduction theories was made by Paul Willis (1977, 1981), whose ethnographic work with "lads" in England, *Learning to Labor: How Working Class Kids Get Working Class Jobs*, expanded the narrow interpretation of the role of schools that Bowles and Gintis and Bourdieu and Passeron had developed.

Willis claimed that schools, besides being places that mirror the economic relations of society and reproduce the dominant culture, are also sites of contestation and counterhegemonic practices. He argued that the reproduction of the values of the dominant society was not a perfect cycle, but on the contrary, students resist the hegemonic discourse at schools.

Through his ethnographic research, Willis documented how students expressed dissatisfaction with the system through unruly behavior and a celebration of masculinity. However, he also found out that the opposition to the middle-class ideology was self-destructive and detrimental to the students' social mobility. Willis concluded that ironically, with this negative resistance, students were contributing to the success of class hierarchy and division of labor.

Willis's seminal ethnographic research on cultural production and *resistance* set the stage for the development of critical ethnography. Willis was the first one to document the *processes* through which social and cultural reproduction occur, but more importantly, he was the first to argue and demonstrate "how education is actually implicated in producing the opposite of the 'liberal hope,' in producing inequality" (Willis, 1981, p. 205).

Willis's theory of cultural production contributed to the understanding of *how* and *why* education has failed:

> [It] is *exactly* the group of kids—those who are the target of a reformist, liberal approach, and who most need to be recruited to the new opportunities if education is to justify its role—who most actively and vociferously reject education. Second, it helps to suggest that far from being "ignorant," "anachronistic," "pathological," and in need of eradication, such cultural responses may in certain important respects be *in advance* of the understanding of the liberal agencies. (Willis, 1981, p. 205)

However, Willis clearly sought to distant himself from Bowles and Gintis (1976) and from Bourdieu and Passeron (1977) by claiming his work was about *cultural production* and not about the static and rigid transmission of correspondence theories.

The second group of scholars from the New Sociology of Education (Anyon, 1980; Apple & King, 1977; Giroux, 1981; Giroux & Pena, 1979; Giroux & Purpel, 1983) moved beyond the examination of schools as agencies of socialization to address the nature of the knowledge taught in schools and its highly ideological composition. "Schools came to be seen as social sites with a dual curriculum: one overt and formal, the other hidden and informal" (Giroux, 1983, p. 45).

Michael Apple and Henry Giroux were the leading theorists of the "hidden curriculum" approach and some of the most influential scholars in the development of the New Sociology of Education. Though they initially were part of the correspondence theorists (particularly with Bowles and Gintis), they later revised their theoretical positionality and began working with another group of North American scholars to set the foundation of what is currently known as critical pedagogy (Apple, 1978; Apple & Weis, 1983; Aronowitz, 1981; Giroux, 1983; McLaren, 1993, 1994).

These critical scholars contended that reproduction theories were narrow interpretations of the complex nature of the schooling system, and that it was inappropriate to reduce schooling to a "dependent variable in the structure of social reproduction" (Aronowitz, 1981, p. vi) without taking into account the dynamics of power and resistance at schools.

These criticalists later developed a more thoughtful foundation of a theory of agency and resistance that, along with the seminal work of Paulo Freire, became the solid ground through which critical pedagogy evolved.

CRITICAL PEDAGOGY

It was during the early 1980s[1] that critical pedagogy emerged as a synthesizer of a variety of radical theories on education. Very few theoretical paradigms have been nurtured from such a range of epistemological currents and academic encounters as critical pedagogy. Critical pedagogy offers an alternative view of schooling that is grounded in the Gramscian concepts of *hegemony* and *ideology*, in the Foucauldian notion of *power* as a dynamic and dialectical process, in the Benjaminian[2] notion of *transformation* and *hope*, and in the Freirian work on conscientization, dialogue, reflection, and praxis.

Critical pedagogy offers an analysis of how hegemony is organized and maintained, how resistance to the dominant societal values is expressed, and how these oppositional attitudes can be transformed into positive counterhegemonic practices for the creation of emancipatory educational experiences.

Critical pedagogy challenges the "positivistic, ahistorical, and depoliticized view of schooling" (McLaren, 1994, p. 167; McLaren & Giarelli, 1995) by unmasking the political and economic nature of education and the contradictions of the very foundations of American traditional pedagogy, such as the notions of equality and meritocracy (Darder, 1991).

Morrow and Torres (1995) describes four major contributions of critical pedagogy to a radical theory of education:

> (1) [It formulates] a theory of cultural reproduction that draws upon the insights of both the Gramscian theory of hegemony and the Frankfurt theory of domination and preserves the essential insights of reproduction theory;
> (2) [it couples] this theory of cultural reproduction in education with an analysis of resistance and social movements capable of grasping the range of potential sources of transformative action;
> (3) [it responds] to the challenge of poststructuralist and postmodernist theories with respect to the limits of social theory and the novel features of the cultural context of advanced capitalism; and
> (4) [it articulates] a theory of the state and political practice oriented toward a conception of democratic populism. (p. 309)

There are four major themes around which critical pedagogy is conceptualized. They are (1) theory of hegemony and social reproduction; (2)

resistance and social transformation; (3) poststructuralist approach to education; and (4) a theory of the state and political practices. However, this book will limit its analysis to the first two categories.

THEORY OF HEGEMONY AND SOCIAL REPRODUCTION: HEGEMONY, IDEOLOGY, AND THE ECONOMY

If there is an area where the work of Antonio Gramsci is clearly manifested, it is in these principles of critical pedagogy. The rediscovery of Gramsci (1971) by Althusser (1969), Laclau (1979), and Stuart Hall and Bram Gieben (1992) allowed critical pedagogy to reclaim Gramsci's legacy and develop the foundation of a radical theory of education.

Gramsci's reconceptualization of Marxist theory has been invaluable in multiple aspects. First, Gramsci captured the sophistication and complexities of the process of social reproduction by transcending the traditional Marxist analysis of social structures and by paying more attention to the processes and subjects participating in that dynamic.

Second, he reduced, without discarding, the economic emphasis of Marxist analysis and infused his theory of "cultural hegemony" with a more humanist, Hegelian vision of social transformation. Third, he deconstructed the process of social reproduction by naming the multiple actors and institutions responsible in the process of class stratification. By doing so, he made these social institutions accountable, particularly schools and their teachers.

In order to understand how the process of social reproduction occurs, it is imperative to know how the concepts of *ideology, hegemony, and economics* are intertwined to produce oppressive social practices. *Ideology* signifies the political discourse and orientation of any social group. It is the system of beliefs, ideas, practices, and ways of interpreting the world. It represents the core values of individuals and social groups, including the dominant society. The successful transmission of the ideology of the dominant society is what ensures its existence and the preservation of the hegemonic classes.

Hegemony is the process through which the ideology of the dominant groups is legitimized, transmitted, and later internalized by the entire society with the consensus of the very social groups that this particular ideology keeps oppressed:

> The dominant culture is able to exercise domination over subordinate classes or groups through a process known as hegemony. Hegemony refers to the maintenance of domination not by the sheer exercise of force but primarily through consensual social practices, social forms, and social structures produced in specific sites such as the church, the state, the school, the mass media, the political system, and the family . . . hegemony is a struggle in which the powerful win the consent of

those who are oppressed, with the oppressed unknowingly participating in their own oppression. (McLaren, 1994, p. 182)

Critical pedagogy has also embraced one of the tenets of Marxist theory, the role of the *economy*, which is a very important principle in this axis of reproduction. Critical pedagogy argues that the economy shapes the ideology of a society and influences every social institution. Because capitalism naturally creates an unequal distribution of resources and generates oppressive social practices, the dominant groups are able to naturalize and mask those unfair consequences by creating values and beliefs (ideology) that are transmitted uncritically by schools and social institutions (hegemony).

For example, the ideology of the hard-work ethic and meritocracy allows society to blame the victims when people are not able to succeed socially or economically because of the way the economy shapes school policies, labor laws, glass ceilings, or other societal constrains. The economy also plays a commanding role in determining school policies and curriculum, and it drives the movement to privatize public schooling.

Therefore, the assumption that schools are the major mechanisms for the development of a democratic and egalitarian social order is a myth (Giroux, 1988). Schools neither promote equal opportunity nor social mobility. They are actually implicated in the process of labor and class stratification, and their educational practices are defined by the interest of the global economic order.

THEORY OF RESISTANCE AND SOCIAL TRANSFORMATION

One of the major contributions of critical pedagogy to the field of critical educational theory is the notion of hope and social agency that was ignored in previous radical approaches to education. The view that the process of social reproduction is a very efficient process where oppressed social groups are incapable of opposing the hegemonic discourse was very detrimental to the notion of social transformation.

It is here where critical pedagogy clearly overcame the theoretical paralysis of correspondence theories by providing a framework for concrete transformative practices. Critical pedagogy integrates the Foucauldian's and Habermas's notion of *historicity of knowledge* as a platform for social and political transformation.

Critical pedagogy uncovers the relationship between knowledge and power, and unmasks—as part of a deconstruction process advocated by Paulo Freire (*dialogue and conscientização*), how knowledge has been presented as universal truth when it is in fact another social construction that has been created by hegemonic groups to keep some social groups in a state of subordination.

Critical pedagogy advocates an examination of the nature of knowledge, the process of knowledge production, and the exclusion of subjugated knowledge—the experiences and histories of marginalized groups that have been excluded from the official curriculum. As McLaren (1994) contends,

> Knowledge acquired in school—or anywhere, for that matter—is never neutral or objective but is ordered and structured in particular ways; its emphasis and exclusions partake of a silent logic. Knowledge is a social construction deeply rooted in a nexus of power relations. (p. 178)

Critical pedagogy argues that only by deconstructing the process and content of the hegemonic discourse through *dialogue* can oppressed social groups become aware of how their consent is used by the dominant society to keep its power and control (*critical consciousness or conscientização*).

Another pivotal tenet of critical pedagogy is the principle of *theory and dialectical thinking* influenced by Hegel's Dialectical Theory of Negativity and developed by Herbert Marcuse (1960). According to the Frankfurt School, theories are neither value-free nor objective; they are social constructions that reflect people's ideologies and beliefs.

A dialectical view of theory offers the possibility of unmasking the contradictions of its tenets (theoretical reconstruction), and the possibility of using these frameworks to expose social contradictions, create awareness, and provide alternative interpretations. A critical view of theory is fundamental in the process of critical consciousness.

According to the Frankfurt School (Giroux, 1983), another constitutive element of theory is that

> it must develop the capacity for meta-theory. That is, it must acknowledge the value-laden interests it represents and be able to reflect critically on both, the historical development or genesis of such interests and the limitations they may present within certain historical and social contexts. (p. 17)

In other words, a critical theory should reflect its unmasking function: "A great truth wants to be criticized, not idolized" (quoted in Arato & Gebhardt, 1978), hence, the necessary principle of dialectical thinking. A dialectical view of the world enables people to move beyond the false dichotomies that positivism has created to reduce knowledge to binary categories and labels.

Dialectical thinking unmasks the false opposition between theory and practice. Historically, theory has been considered the domain of a privileged elite that has controlled the process of knowledge production, particularly conventional scientific research. In contrast, the practitioner, the activist, and the laborer have the power of experience, but their knowledge is deemed inferior because they have been told they lack the capacity to formulate theories or engage in "scientific" research.

This false dichotomy between theory and practice is not innocent at all. It legitimizes class stratification and prevents subordinated groups from critiquing and confronting the structures of domination that keep them subordinated. As Giroux argues (1983),

> The value of any experience "will depend not on the experience of the subject but on the struggles around the way that experience is interpreted and defined" (Bennett, 2002). Moreover, theory cannot be reduced to being perceived as the mistress of experience, empowered to provide recipes for pedagogical practice. Its real value lies in its ability to establish possibilities for reflexive thought and practice on the part of those who use it [. . .] it becomes invaluable as an instrument of critique and understanding. (p. 21)

The understanding of that dialectical relationship is fundamental for the development of historical consciousness and the formulation of praxis.

The principle of *praxis* synthesizes the belief of critical pedagogy that all transformative actions are the outcome of the synergetic relationship between theory, experience, dialogue, and reflection. Praxis, unlike practice, is not a simple activity, but a committed decision to engage in the transformation of the world as a result of dialogue, reflection, and critical consciousness, all facilitated by a critical reading of theory.

Freire (1970) defines praxis as "reflection and action upon the world in order to transform it" (p. 33). He contends that, through praxis, "oppressed people can acquire a critical awareness of their own condition, and, with their allies, struggle for liberation" (p. 36).

The principles of *resistance and counterhegemony* emerged from Gramsci's theory of cultural hegemony and are the most distinctive tenets of critical pedagogy. In fact, the formulation of a theory of resistance and social agency was the breakthrough of critical pedagogy and one of the most important contributions to the field of critical educational theory.

It advanced the notion that the reproduction of the dominant society ideology is not a perfect process, but on the contrary, subordinated groups resist and confront the hegemonic cycle. This was something that was not contemplated in previous approaches, particularly reproduction theories.

This theory of resistance and social agency moved forward by critical pedagogy uncovers the conflicting relationship between hegemonic and oppressed social groups. It articulates how hegemony is not a perfect process and confirms that subordinated groups are not uncritically and submissively accepting their domination. Critical pedagogy offers a broader picture of the complex dynamic through which oppressed social groups explicitly and tacitly resist the dominant social order. This vision is based on the following concepts:

1. The reproduction of the hegemonic discourse and its correspondent oppressive social practices is not a flawless process. Subordinated social groups tacitly and explicitly resist oppressive mechanisms of coercion and consensus.
2. The reaction of marginalized groups to the dominant social order varies according to their level of "cultural response and mode of engagement" (Darder, 1991, p. 58). Their responses range from alienation and dualism to separatism and negotiation.
3. Certain "modes of engagement" and resistance of oppressed social groups to the dominant social order might contribute to the success of the dominant social order (see Willis's study on cultural production). Therefore, a theory of resistance and social agency makes a distinction between self-destructive mechanisms of resistance and transformative counterhegemonic practices.
4. Through dialogue, reflection, and critical consciousness, subordinated groups can learn how to funnel their oppositional behaviors (resistance) into counterhegemonic practices that can successfully contest the dominant social order while retaining their human agency, transformative potential, social mobility, and ability to sustain and defend their communities.

TRANSFORMATIVE PRACTICES

Critical pedagogy advocates for the development of critical consciousness that leads to a cultural politics that upholds a critical discourse. A *critical discourse* formulates an alternative perspective to the sanctioned dominant discourse. It articulates a counternarrative on how power is constructed; it unmasks what discourses are acknowledged, what truths are spoken and legitimized, and which ones are silenced.

Grounded on the Foucauldian notion of discursive practices and Habermas's study on communication patterns, a critical discourse problematizes the ideological underpinnings that shape language, speech, and communication styles and its relationship to power. Particularly, a critical discourse advocates for an examination of the *standard* discursive practices in schools, speech patterns, and writing styles, and their role in silencing the voices of marginalized social groups.

CONSCIENTIZAÇÃO

The two most significant contributions of Paulo Freire to critical pedagogy are the principles of *dialogue and critical consciousness*, which are essential elements for the development of a critical discourse. These two tenets offer concrete strategies for political activism and reposition this pedagogy from a language of denouncement and resistance to a language of social transformation.

It is through dialogue—problem-posing pedagogy—that all the other concepts of critical pedagogy are deconstructed—ideology, hegemony, resistance, economics, historicity of knowledge, dialectical thinking, theory, praxis, and cultural politics. Darder asserts that this "dialogical method represents the basis for a critical pedagogical structure in which dialogue and analysis serve as the foundation for reflection and action" (p. 94).

One of the major challenges to a true implementation of critical pedagogy derives from the capacity to make dialogue and *conscientization* an essential component of a truly liberatory educational practice.

NOTES

1. This was a time in North America when liberalism began to fall. The attacks of the New Left were complemented by the attacks of a new and stronger New Right. Wexler (1987) argues that radical educators were so concerned about dismantling the myths of liberalism that they left the doors open for a reemergence of conservatism. "The radical educational discourse that had been fueled as an historical negation of liberalism was unprepared to find liberalism on the run, under attack from a powerful New Right" (p. 42).

2. Walter Benjamin was one of the most prominent members of the Frankfurt School.

THREE

The Ideological Predicament of Teacher Education

THE IDEOLOGICAL STATE APPARATUS

One of the greatest contributions of Louis Althusser[1] to the field of critical educational theory was the development of a theory of ideology that explains how capitalist societies perpetuate and impose their values over the working class. Unlike Karl Marx who focused on the role of the economy, Althusser addressed the social structures that are responsible for the enactment and reproduction of the dominant society ideology (Wolff, 2005).

Influenced by Gramsci (1971), Althusser believes that the maintenance of the existing system of production and power arrangements depends on both the use of force and the use of ideology. For him, the reproduction of the "conditions of production" rests upon three important interrelated moments: 1) the production of values that support the relations of production; 2) the use of force and ideology to support the dominant classes in all important spheres of control; and 3) the production of knowledge and skills relevant to specific forms of work (Althusser, 1971, p. 79).

Althusser identified two sites—social structures—where the enactment and transmission of the ideological values of capitalism occur. They are (1) the *repressive* state apparatuses, which is limited to the state and its offices, and (2) the *ideological* state apparatuses where the procurement of consensus is manufactured, mostly in social institutions.

Gramsci conceptualized the first social structure—the *repressive* state apparatus—as the one implicated in the process of coercion. This role is carried out by the state and its offices and is fundamental for the compulsory enforcement of the rules and values of the dominant society. The actions of the *repressive* state apparatus are seen in the activities of law enforcement agencies, judicial systems, legislative bodies, and so forth.

Gramsci had also identified the second site, the *ideological* state apparatus, in the work of some of the most important institutions in society, such as schools, family, religious groups, and the media. It is in these social organizations where the ideology of the market is discreetly enacted, reinforced, and reproduced, and where the procurement of consent takes place.

Althusser believed that these *ideological* state apparatuses "do more than create subjectivities/identities in the individuals whom they interpellate. They also aim to have such subjects imagine that their subjectivities/identities are internally self-generated" (Wolff, 2005, p. 5). When individuals pledge allegiance to the values and beliefs of the dominant society, they do so believing they are doing it out of their own personal conviction and free will, without understanding how the ideological state apparatuses have prepared them to accept those beliefs as their personal and deliberate choices.

In sum, according to Althusser, ideology is not a conscious activity or rational condition, but rather an unconscious process that develops from childhood and continues through the daily life of the individual. Ideology is constantly formed and reinforced through rituals and social interaction in the family, schools, churches, and the media. Ideology is a system of representation made of images and concepts that have particular values, and these ideological apparatuses are sites where that system of representation acquires concrete meaning.

Schools are the primary social institutions implicated in the ideological control of subordinated groups (Bernstein, 1971–1975, 1977), and they do so while portraying a humanist vision about the redemptive and transformative power of education. This is what Giroux (1981) describes as the "paradox of education" (p. 143) and Popkewitz (1987) calls the "social predicament of schooling."

UNMASKING THE CONSERVATIVE NATURE OF TEACHER EDUCATION

Structuralism, poststructuralism, the new sociology of education, and critical pedagogy have identified teacher education as one of the ideological state apparatuses implicated in the production and transmission of capitalist values. Teacher education is the place where the hegemonic procurement of consent is carried out through the inculcation of the essential knowledge and skills that support the power arrangement of the larger society (Althusser, 1971; Derrida, 1977; Foucault, 1980; Giroux, 1980; Giroux & McLaren, 1988; Morrow & Torres, 1995; Popkewitz, 1984).

Teacher education programs are not neutral institutions as they operate and enact administrative and curricular practices that protect the economic and social interest of the ruling class (Giroux, 1980, p. 12). An examination of "whose culture gets distributed in [teacher education], who benefits from such culture" (Giroux, 1980, p. 12), "who benefits by the methods of teaching, [. . .] and the way student teaching is structured" (Beyer & Zeichner, 1987, p. 2), clearly expose that the "*sacred* knowledge that is communicated overtly and covertly in teacher education is in fact value-governed" (Beyer & Zeichner, 1987, p. 313).

There have been three theoretical movements in teacher education that have influenced its ideology and the way teachers learn to teach. They are (1) traditionalism, (2) rationalism, and (3) radicalism. Traditionalism views teaching as a craft that is passed down to new generations through an apprenticeship model. In this tradition the focus of teacher preparation is the socialization and induction of teachers (Kirk, 1986).

Rationalism emerged as a response to traditionalism and sees teaching as an applied science and the mastery of skills and lesson plans. Radicalism disputes both traditionalism and rationalism and proposes a reexamination of teaching beyond the educational psychology confines to attend and reflect on the political nature of schooling (Apple, 1993; Giroux, 1980; Giroux & McLaren, 1988; Kincheloe, Steinberg & Villaverde, 1999; Shor, 1986).

However, the dominant ideology of teacher education is rationalism. Teacher education is deeply influenced by the psychological models of the Industrial Revolution that made scientific management and control one of the greatest successes in the advancement of capitalism. That is the reason why the technical and managerial view of schools is reinforced through the entire formation of teachers (Giroux, 1980, p. 14). The themes of control, methodologies, efficiency, testing, and standardization are persistently encouraged:

> Instead of learning to raise questions about the principles underlying different classroom methods, research techniques and theories of education, students [teachers] are often preoccupied with learning the "how to," with "what works," or with mastering the best way to teach a "given" body of knowledge. (Giroux, 1988, p. 124)

Thus, if ideology refers to "the production of sense and meaning [. . .] a way of viewing the world, a complex of ideas, various types of social practices, rituals, and representations that we tend to accept as natural and as common sense" (McLaren, 1994, p. 184), teacher education is full of hegemonic messages and rites. These rituals are infused in the curriculum and in the *commonsense* practices of teacher education. They are embedded in the codes of conduct, categories of discourse, and "regimes of truth" (Foucault, 1977) that are part of the preparation of teachers.

What follows is an articulation of the premises that govern teacher education departments and constitute the ideology of teacher preparation programs:

- Psychological theories dominate the explanation of effective teaching practices and learning (Beyer & Zeichner, 1987; Giroux, 1980; Greene, 1984; Nussbaum, 2010; Popkewitz, 1987). There is an overreliance on behaviorist pedagogical models of social control to foment docile and conformist students. These pedagogical models are recommended to teachers to deal with students living in poverty, immigrants, children with disabilities, and minorities (Giroux, 1980, p. 14; Haberman, 1988, 1995; Payne, 2003).
- Teacher education skillfully selects educational theories to justify the practice of "sorting, classifying, [evaluating and standardizing] that makes the ongoing relations of school seem normal" (Popkewitz, 1987, p. 17). In reality, "theories are social inventions [that can be used] for action and rituals of social manipulation" (p. 19).
- Teacher education emphasizes the primacy of practice at the expense of theory, which has the function of reducing teaching to a method to "desensitize new teachers to the social and political contradictions of the curriculum in a differentiated society" (Popkewitz, 1987, p. 17). Teacher education reinforces the vision of teachers as classroom managers and test proctors rather than teachers as advocates, intellectuals, or researchers.
- Mass schooling from the industrialization era dominates teacher education's vision of public education. "Schools are seen as factories and students as raw materials" (Giroux, 1980, p. 14). In spite of the rhetoric of differentiated instruction and inclusiveness, students are still taught using the banking concept of education (Freire, 1994), and schools are seldom visualized as "little democracies" (Dewey, 1916).
- Teacher education reinforces the assumed impartiality and universality of the official knowledge that is taught in teacher preparation, leaving no possibility to question the curricular and pedagogical choices (Giroux, 1980; Popkewitz, 1979, 1991, 1993, 1997).
- Teacher education is an important participant in the manipulation of symbols and rituals that naturalize questionable educational practices. For example, "Nation at Risk [No Child Left Behind, and Race to the Top] can also be viewed as part of a public ceremony that structures policy in ways that [. . .] shape public perception about economic priorities" (Popkewitz, 1987, p. 18).
- Teacher education promotes socialization models among faculty and students that are based on a consensus discourse that disguise the underlying power struggles and economic alliances of teacher education programs (Giroux, 1980, p. 16).

These discourses inform the pedagogical knowledge that students learn at teacher preparation programs. Teachers later translate these discourses into detrimental teaching practices, reproducing in this way the ideology of the dominant society. Some of these questionable teaching practices are:

- A vertical—and very often authoritarian—relationship between students and teachers that resembles the relationship of the labor force (Popkewitz, 1987, p. 3).
- Grouping and tracking practices that reinforce notions of inferiority on working-class children and students of color, negating the possibilities for social mobility (Darder, 1991; McLaren, 1994).
- A glorification of the official knowledge that is unquestionably and homogeneously delivered without any deconstruction of its hidden agenda, and without any examination of the experiences that are excluded (Anyon, 1980, 1981; Apple, 1979, 1982; Foucault, 1977; Giroux, 1980, 1981; Giroux & McLaren, 1987, 1988).
- A strong reliance on standardized tests and other psychometric instruments to appraise students' intelligence and learning, without any discussion of the political function of testing and its role in the selection of the "social fittest" (Darder, 1991; Kincheloe, Steinberg & Villaverde, 1999).
- An irrational emphasis on assessment and accountability that is manifested in the obsessive testing of students (Giroux, 1988; Popkewitz, 1987).
- A glorification of meritocracy suggesting that hard work pays off, as manifested in the rituals of differentiation: "award ceremonies, tests, grades, compensatory education, gifted education, and school scores" (Popkewitz, 1987, pp. 23–24).
- Homework policies that penalize working-class students and their parents but serve the purpose of confirming the "social predicament of schooling" (Popkewitz, 1987).
- Cultural invisibility of the students and their families as manifested in their absence in the curriculum and school decision-making process.
- Imposition of an official "knowledge [that is] separated from the lives of teachers, students and their families" constituting a form of "pedagogical violence" (Giroux, 1980, p. 19).

These schemes constitute the foundation of the logic of social reproduction and are part of what Popkewitz (1987) calls "rituals of differentiation and homogeneity" in teacher education. Under this ideology, there is no discussion in teacher preparation about issues of power and domination, or about the role that teachers play in the reproduction of the dominant society's discourse.

On the contrary, by ignoring "the relationship between power and school knowledge, [teacher educators] often end up celebrating in both the overt and hidden curricula, knowledge that support existing institutional arrangement" (Giroux, 1980, p. 19). This ideology constitutes the cultural and ideological background of aspirant teachers due to their own schooling experience and their formation at teacher preparation programs.

TEACHERS AS TRANSFORMATIVE INTELLECTUALS

Informed by the most important principles of critical pedagogy—resistance and social agency—Giroux (1980) proposes to reclaim teacher preparation programs as public spheres where teachers learn a "dialectical language [. . .] and the conceptual tools they need in order to view knowledge [and their role] as problematic" (p. 19). He believes there are political spaces and relative autonomy in teacher education that offer the possibility of transforming teacher preparation and the teaching profession:

> Teacher education programs operate within parameters that are severely constraining, but they also contain options for creating new possibilities and social realities [. . .] the seeds exist within teacher education for developing "critical intellectuals" who can begin the task of generating a more radical and visionary consciousness among their fellow workers, friends, and students. (Giroux, 1980, p. 20)

In opposition to the arguments against radicalism, critical pedagogy does conceptualize a concrete framework for authentically transforming the preparation of teachers and reclaiming schools as "little democracies." What critical pedagogy does not elaborate is how to implement this framework, as that would be to fall into the trap of the rationalism argument (Steinberg & Kincheloe, 1998).

Nonetheless, what follows are some of the recommendations to authentically transform teacher education based on a critical pedagogical framework:

- Teacher education must offer students "theoretical and methodological tools to examine and critique naturalized but oppressive power arrangements of the larger society" (Giroux, 1980, p. 21). For example, students must learn the role of schooling in supporting the dominant society and excluding subordinated social groups (Beyer, 1989; Nussbaum, 2001, 2006).
- Teacher education must teach and deconstruct "critical categories for educational theory and practice like social class, ideology, false consciousness and hegemony. These categories must be linked to

oppression, emancipation, freedom and indoctrination" (Giroux, 1980, p. 21).

- Teacher education must teach that schools resemble the structures, processes, and "relationship of the workplace and other agencies of socialization and social control" (Giroux, 1980, p. 21).
- Teacher education must provide theories and practices that unveil that "knowledge is a socio political construction and methodological inquiry is never value-free" (Giroux, 1980, p. 21). For example, student teachers must oppose the banking concept of education, and they must be able to question the knowledge that is being taught and the knowledge they will be teaching (Beyer, 1989).
- Teacher education must provide structures and processes that encourage student teachers to develop their own voice (Giroux, 1980, p. 21). For example, the use of problem-posing pedagogy and dialogical teaching must be essential in teacher education courses (Shor, 1992).
- Teacher education must include a mandatory component of social justice and social action in its curriculum, service learning, and field placement (Giroux, 1980; Nussbaum, 2006, 2010).
- Teacher education must provide the personal, political, and academic spaces for "deeper self awareness and justice that link the biographical with the social and the private with the community" (Giroux, 1980, p. 21; Greene, 1978, p. 70; Weiner, 1993).
- Teacher education must provide the spaces for students to "delve into their own biographies" to understand their ideological positionality and the interplay of their histories and their teaching (Giroux, 1980, p. 23).
- Teacher education must provide the opportunity for teacher educators, administrators, and student teachers to teach, learn, and practice how to think dialectically and to develop a theory of totality (Giroux, 1980). Sharp and Green (1975) develop this concept further:

> To ask for a theory of totality is to ask how a society reproduces itself, how it perpetuates its conditions of existence through its reproduction of class relationship and its propagation of ideologies, which sanction the status quo (p. 221).

- Teacher education must organize its curriculum and student teachers' pedagogical experiences based on a dialectical view of teaching: academic knowledge has to be related, contrasted, and explained in light of the larger power arrangements. One of the outcomes of that dialectical thinking would be to provide fluidity among subject matters and learning experiences (Giroux, 1980, p. 22).

- Teacher education must be interdisciplinary and integrate other disciplines like "history, sociology, anthropology, economics, and philosophy as essential components of the formation of teachers" (Greene, 1978, p. 59; Nussbaum, 2010).
- Teacher education must offer other theoretical models rather than relying exclusively on educational psychology. For example, students must be offered the opportunity to deconstruct the *psychologization* of schooling (Beyer, 1989).
- Teacher education must provide teaching and learning in "different languages and different rationalities, e.g., technical, political, scientific, aesthetic, and ethical" (Giroux, 1980, p. 23).

These suggestions for the transformation of teacher preparation do not exclude the recommendations of other scholars who focus on the way teacher education is structured, and how the field experience and inquiry process is integrated in the education of teachers (Cochran-Smith & Fries, 2001; Cochran-Smith & Lytle; 1993; Darling-Hammond, 1985; Darling-Hammond, Wise & Klein, 1995; Zeichner, 2006).

Darling-Hammond (1998), in particular, offers some specific advice on what makes good teachers and what makes exemplary teacher education programs:

What makes good teachers?

1. a coherent curriculum that tightly intertwines theory and practice
2. field work that is integrated with classwork, coupled with support from carefully selected mentors
3. an extended clinical component with a minimum of thirty weeks of student teaching
4. an emphasis on learning theory and child development, with extensive training in the ability to address the needs of diverse learners (p. 10)

What are the characteristics of exemplary teacher preparation programs?

- a common, clear vision of good teaching that permeates all coursework and clinical experiences, creating a coherent set of learning experiences
- well-defined standards of professional practice and performance that are used to guide and evaluate coursework and clinical work
- a strong core curriculum taught in the context of practice and grounded in the knowledge of child and adolescent development and learning, an understanding of social and cultural contexts, curriculum, assessment, and subject matter pedagogy
- extended clinical experiences: at least thirty weeks of supervised practicum and student teaching opportunities in each program— that are carefully chosen to support the ideas presented in simultaneous, closely interwoven coursework

- extensive use of case methods, teacher research, performance assessment, and portfolio evaluation that apply learning to real problems of practice
- explicit strategies to help students to confront their own deep-seated beliefs and assumptions about learning and students and to learn about the experiences of people different from themselves
- strong relationships, common knowledge, and shared beliefs among school- and university-based faculty jointly engaged in transforming teaching, schooling, and teacher education (Darling-Hammond, 2006, p. 305)

OTHER ATTEMPTS TO TRANSFORM TEACHER EDUCATION

There is not enough literature documenting authentic efforts to change the culture of teacher education. Two case studies appeared more conceptually related to the experience described in this book. One of such efforts occurred at a small, private college on the East Coast where the faculty along with some administrators decided to challenge the dominant paradigm in their teacher education department.

This group of university professors aimed to raise issues of social inequality, social justice, and political and ethical action in their education department with the intention of preparing teachers to become scholars, curricular designers, pedagogues, and activists (Beyer, 1989, p. 22). Their recommendations ranged from a change in the name of the teacher preparation department to Educational Studies (p. 23) to the creation of a new academic major.

The curriculum was reconceptualized with a significant integration of philosophy and educational foundations courses. Special attention was paid to the sequence of the courses, the organization of the experience, and the student admission criteria. Although some of the changes were gradually being implemented, the final decision rested in a college subcommittee and the state department for further approval.

Ironically, the state agency was ready to offer temporary authorization of the program, but not the university, who, represented by the subcommittee, resisted any major change. The rejection of the proposed changes was justified under "liberal/technical proceduralism" (Beyer, 1989, p. 24). However, the objection was based on a more substantive issue: the liberal ideology that sees teaching as a discipline involved in the production of pure knowledge and removed from any political and ideological context.

The anti-intellectualism of the teacher education faculty became evident in the discussion of the teacher education curriculum; particularly, the proposal to include philosophy and educational foundation courses into the teacher education curriculum. Questions were raised about the use of the words *ideology, aesthetic,* and *epistemology,* but in the end, the rejection of the transformation to the teacher education program was justified for economic reasons. Beyer (1989) explains:

> One might expect that a primary concern of such review committees would be the effect of our proposals on students. And this was the case. Yet "the concern" manifested did not center on the academic appropriateness of our courses and programs, or on how they would affect the ability of students to become effective teachers. Instead, there was a great deal of apprehension expressed over the consequences for enrollment and attrition . . . and enrollment projections [. . .] Such concerns are not completely unwarranted, of course, especially in small, private liberal arts colleges where tuition payments represent a sizeable portion of the operating budget. Nevertheless, in substituting market values and technical/liberal proceduralism for intellectual engagement and debate the college did not exemplify the very traditions of inquiry it alleged to uphold. (pp. 24–25)

Lastly, the proposal to transform the teacher education department was rejected, and the faculty who had authored the proposal resigned. The proposed courses were abandoned and others were "reinterpreted through a more technical lens." The teacher education program went back to a more conservative stance at the same time that the previous rigorous admission criteria were removed (Beyer, 1989, p. 25).

The second case study found in the literature refers to a teacher education program for social justice at West Coast University. The authors, who were simultaneously doctoral students and teacher education faculty, created pedagogical and political spaces in one foundation course to explore the seriousness of the social justice commitment of their department.

Using inquiry as a methodological and theoretical approach (Dewey, Smyth, Freire, Giroux & McLaren), the researchers assessed the social justice commitment of the program. They were pleased with the political space provided to the teacher-interns in that course, but they realized the students could not become transformative intellectuals just by getting their credential in the program.

The researchers were able to demonstrate how inquiry could be used as an alternative pedagogical model to raise political awareness. However, they concluded, the effort to transform a teacher education program develops from a more coherent and interrelated effort to bring the political into the academic and the personal into the professional.

NOTE

1. Althusser's "Ideology and Ideological State Apparatuses" constitutes one of the most refined developments of Gramsci's theory of hegemony. See Althusser, 1971.

FOUR

The Teacher Education Program at Laurel Canyon University

SECTION I: THE TOWN, THE UNIVERSITY

Laurel Canyon University[1] is located in a small college town surrounded by a conglomerate of several blue-collar cities. These communities are not the classic California suburban areas. They appear economically depressed and slightly middle class, but they all have in common that they are very diverse. Their population reflects the faces and the cultures of the new Californians, mostly people from minority backgrounds. However, the city of Laurel Canyon is very different. It is an upper-middle-class enclave that is hidden in the middle of a very racially and economically diverse community.

The beauty of the campus and the city is striking. Located at the foothills of some of the most gorgeous mountain ranges in California, this picturesque college town looks immaculate and peaceful, as if time had stopped there. It seems the perfect place for contemplation and study, the ideal setting for a university.

People do not know where the town begins and the university ends. The city park appears to be part of the university, and the university pools are well attended by the community, particularly during the summer. People know and greet each other; they stroll, run errands, go to the park with their kids, and have coffee downtown. However, they also attend lectures, concerts, and visit art galleries at the university.

Both the university and the town share the beautifully manicured lawns tendered by the ever-present Latino gardeners. The university also owns some of the expensive and well-preserved Craftsman houses that adorn the neighborhood. They also share the enormous, fronded trees that decorate the streets. During the summer, these immense, splendid trees provide protection to walk in the hot temperatures of the area. This smooth architectural integration of the university and the city is what attracts most visitors and makes the lives of the students and the people of Laurel Canyon comfortable.

Fall is the prettiest season of the year in Laurel Canyon. The leaves of the trees turn into a stunning palette of orange, brown, yellow, purple, and red colors that offer a unique glimpse of autumn so rarely experienced in California. During one of the famous storms in the area, a couple of eucalyptus trees fell down and killed two students who were parking their car on the street on their way to their dormitories. It was a very tragic event that symbolized the symbiotic relationship between the university and the town.

However, there were some deep fissures between the townspeople, the students, and their professors. Some of the conflicts were common to other towns where college people impose their lifestyle on the grown-up residents. There was also the common clash between young, idealistic students versus the all-White, middle-age, upper-class townspeople who managed the city and the law enforcement agencies. The other conflicts were related to what the town residents, and even the university, perceived as the threat caused by the most racially and economically disenfranchised population that lived in the nearby communities.

The city and university police worked in unison to protect the community from the crime that afflicted the neighbor cities, and they did it by watching out for minority people who appeared to have no business in the community. Elements of racism were widespread during those years. The behavior of the police of Laurel Canyon caught my attention, to such an extent that I began observing in detail every time they stopped a motorist. Coincidentally or not, every time I saw a police person giving a traffic ticket, the driver was a female, a Latino/a, or an African American. It became clear in university circles that the police had a reputation for intimidating people whom they believed did not belong to the community.

In one of the many tragic incidents in the city, the local police killed an African American male who resided in one of the neighboring towns when he drove drunk through the city of Laurel Canyon and failed to stop when required. Tales of similar incidents afflicted the city and incensed students and faculty, who constantly organized demonstrations to bring up the issues to the city council.

Those incidents reflected the ambivalent relationship between the city and the university. The charm of the small town and the sophistication of the academic community concealed the questionable politics and the dirty secrets that protected the seeming serene lifestyle of the city of Laurel Canyon. It is in that context that the teacher preparation program at Laurel Canyon University (LCU) evolved.

SECTION II: KRISTINE AND THE ALL-WHITE BOYS CLUB

Kristine was the first female faculty hired by the College of Education at Laurel Canyon University. Up to that point, the entire faculty body was White, middle-age, male professors who ran the College of Education as their private club. Among the professors were Joseph, the child psychologist; Patrick, the educational foundation faculty; Wayne, the higher education guru; Martin, the qualitative research expert; and Larry, the policy analyst. Kristine was young, savvy, and articulate, and she was able to impress her future colleagues, who quickly embraced her. Kristine gradually rose among the ranks of the faculty at the College of Education, and she gradually began to draw the attention of the rest of the university.

Years later, another faculty was hired at the college: a male, African American professor. After several years of working at LCU, this professor applied for tenure, but his application was denied. He sued the university, arguing that the decision was discriminatory. This professor had obtained evidence of the discussion that took place during the deliberation of his application that apparently conveyed racist policies. He won a settlement against the university after it appeared that the court was going to side with him and Laurel Canyon University wanted to avoid a major embarrassment.

After this incident, LCU launched a major effort to market its commitment to multiculturalism. The College of Education began an effort to diversify the faculty body and remove the image that the media had portrayed about the politics of race at the university. As a result, two new female faculty were hired. They were Sylvia, a Caucasian specialist in higher education, and Teresa, a Latina authority in cultural diversity.

A few years later, the College of Education invited three more professors to join its faculty. They were a renowned African American researcher, a Latina from another department of the university, and a Japanese American male who was a former superintendent of a school district in another city. It was clear that the College of Education had an interest in conveying a strong commitment to diversity. At least, there appeared to be more colored bodies among its faculty.

Kristine was already a senior professor when Teresa and Sylvia were hired. From the reconstituted faculty body at the College of Education, Kristine appeared to be the best positioned and more respected faculty among her male colleagues to succeed, and she was determined to do so. She was the director of the teacher education department, and she was a tall, slender, Caucasian faculty who had a formidable reputation with the university as an excellent administrator. She was the one who modernized the teacher education program and had successfully created a "cash cow" for the university based on a profitable model of teacher preparation.

Kristine ruled teacher education forcefully, like a corporate chief executive officer. She was a powerful woman who counted with the favor of her male colleagues, and particularly, the dean, the provost, and the president of the university. She also relied on the academic and professional contacts she had developed with the neighbor school districts during her long tenure at the College of Education.

Kristine was able to depict her department as one of the exemplary multicultural teacher preparation programs in California. She had marketed herself as a progressive educator whose area of expertise was special education. During her early tenure, Kristine's colleagues and friends knew her as an avant-garde, charismatic woman who was passionate about constructivist theory and cultural diversity. However, in the latter phase of her career she became righteous, and she evolved into an orthodox, religious person.

As a private university, Laurel Canyon attracted undergraduate students who came from very affluent families. However, its graduate programs were more diverse. The College of Education designed its doctorate and master's degree programs for students who worked full time. That is what made the education programs so attractive to students in the area. Kristine had wisely capitalized on this reputation to create one of the two most profitable graduate programs[2] in the entire university.

Kristine had inherited a graduate teacher credential program from her predecessor that offered prospective candidates the possibility of obtaining a master's degree and a teaching credential in fifteen months. While the university charged students approximately $35,000 in tuition per year, Kristine had structured teacher preparation in a model that allowed students to get a full-time job as interns during their second term in the program, and just after a brief student teaching experience.

Kristine was delighted with the popularity of the program, and she bragged about how most of the students were hired by school districts during the student-teaching stage. In fact, about 99 percent of the student teachers obtained full-time teaching jobs during their first semester in the program, and that first year counted toward tenure if their districts retained them.

Most of the aspiring teachers who applied to the teacher education department did so after hearing from another teacher or school administrator who recommended the program for its success. In a time when teachers were quitting the profession at an alarming rate, the graduates of the teacher preparation program at Laurel Canyon University continued teaching successfully even after their fifth year as educators.

There were other important features that made this teacher preparation program unique. Laurel Canyon University prided itself on its small classes and the personalized guidance its students received. The teacher education program exemplified that tradition by admitting an average of one hundred aspirant teachers per year, which created a ratio of seven students per instructor and faculty advisors.

The small-size class feature was highly enhanced with the cohort model. The program admitted students only two times a year, creating in this way very cohesive cohorts of teacher candidates. Students were also placed in small advisory groups led by a faculty supervisor who worked with them during their entire academic program. The support system functioned at three levels: the small-size classroom, the cohort structure, and the advisory groups.

Unlike other apprenticeship programs, students at the teacher preparation program at Laurel Canyon came with previous experience in teaching. That was an admission requirement. Students were placed in very diverse school districts for a very short student-teaching experience (six to ten weeks) under the mentoring of a master teacher at the school and the supervision of a university professor. Most of the student teachers obtained full-time teaching jobs in the summer, and in the fall they began working as teachers with an internship credential under the guidance of the university faculty who visited their classroom on a weekly basis, and a mentor teacher at the school site.

SECTION III: SAMANTHA, THE ASSISTANT PROFESSOR

Samantha began her journey at Laurel Canyon University as a master's degree student pursuing her California teaching credential. After traveling the world as a military wife and working several jobs, including teaching on military bases and community colleges across the nation for eighteen years, she finally settled down in the city of Laurel Canyon.

After obtaining her credential, she taught in the city's exclusive public schools, and later she enrolled in Laurel Canyon's doctoral program. Samantha taught summer courses to preservice teachers at the College of Education, and later it was natural that she became a faculty at the teacher education department. Samantha's experience and affable personality made her one of Kristine's favorite professors.

Samantha quickly rose to the highest administrative ranks as she knew the business of teaching, but more so because she always volunteered to do the work. Kristine loved that attitude and the fact that Samantha's intensive labor released ample time for her to pursue her personal ambitions. Samantha became the assistant director of the teacher education program for three years while Kristine focused her energy on a major grant she had just been awarded to focus on urban education. Samantha's position as the assistant director of teacher preparation was the beginning of an ambivalent relationship between Samantha and Kristine.

Thus, Kristine began a four-year research project aimed at understanding the conditions, dynamics, and experiences of teachers and students in some diverse schools. She contended that she wanted to provide a glimpse of what was going in those classrooms so that teacher preparation could accommodate those situations. In partnership with Patrick, the educational foundation faculty, Kristine created paid positions to run the research project. She appointed her doctoral students and some teacher education faculty as research fellows. She also sought the collaboration of friends and acquaintances from the neighboring schools to assist her in this project.

The publication of this research report catapulted Kristine's reputation. She had finally made a name for herself as a "progressive," "multicultural" teacher educator, who was passionate about special education issues, and who finally had discovered the formula for training excellent teachers. However, it became clear years later, through some of the participants, that this study that consolidated Kristine's position was lacking rigor. There were increasing concerns about the methodology and the use of published academic work that was included as part of the findings of the research project.

Nevertheless, Kristine took a sabbatical for a year to publish a book on that research and was able to use that study to join the ranks of nationally reputable research organizations. At home, at the LCU's College of Education, most of the participants knew how that reputation had been created, and it became clear about Kristine's unstoppable ambitions.

Meanwhile, Samantha kept running the teacher preparation program while finishing her dissertation. She took on the major responsibility of getting the teacher education program accredited at the state level while Kristine was on leave. According to Samantha, during this time she became aware that she could not work under Kristine's leadership any more.

Samantha said she became tired of Kristine's manipulation of faculty and staff, and her newly developed conservative mind-set was becoming a liability for the internship program she had successfully created many years ago. Lately, Kristine has begun expressing antigay statements. Thus, as soon as Samantha got her doctoral degree she resigned to become an assistant professor at another university.

Something had happened to Kristine during her sabbatical year. She became very religious, in an orthodox way, and her newly acquired religious beliefs intensified her hard-core approach. When Kristine returned to the College of Education, she announced that she did not want to continue running the department of teacher education. Students and faculty at the College of Education knew that Kristine wanted to bring Samantha back to become the new director of the program.

SECTION IV: TERESA, THE DIVERSITY FACULTY

Teresa was one of the rising stars at the college of education at Laurel Canyon University (LCU). Her strong personality captivated and intrigued the graduate students. It was unclear what she was doing in that place: all homogenous, mainstream, impeccable, and very conservative. It was still an all-White boys club when she arrived there. However, everyone knew she had graduated from the College of Education, and after several stints at other universities she applied to LCU and was successfully hired. Her appointment occurred a few years later after the dismissal of the African American professor and subsequent settlement.

Teresa had an astonishing ability to denounce and unpeel the comfortable life of the academy.

> "She's brutally honest," one of my colleagues told me.

> "She curses and appears angry," another colleague told me, a white, wealthy academician.

Yet Teresa was powerful, and the students of color worshipped her. She relied on her own experience growing up poor and barefoot in Texas. She remembered raising three children as a single mother while on welfare, and then, working odd jobs to put food in the table. She remembered doing a lot of activism, going to community college, and getting degrees until she finally obtained her doctorate in education.

Faculty and students said that Teresa was always angry. Indeed, she always looked angry, but she said she had more than a million reasons to be angry and resentful. She was supposed to be one of the dropout statistics, but through a difficult journey she became one of the top professors at Laurel Canyon University. What was always impressive about Teresa was her academic and political articulation of what it meant to be a poor, bilingual Latina trying to transcend the boundaries of race and social class.

Teresa was a great role model for the students of color, as they perceived her as providing some sort of protection in the privileged, but at times hostile, environment at LCU. However, Teresa was also intimidating, harsh, and abrasive when students did not agree with her views, and because of that, she missed the opportunity to influence those who desperately needed her guidance.

The same inflexible attitude extended to her relationship with her colleagues. She appeared to have cordial relationships with all the professors, and they tolerated her as long as she did not intrude in their professional and academic lives. However, once they disagreed with her or confronted her, clashes ensued.

Laurel Canyon University used Teresa's charismatic personality and academic credentials to market the College of Education as one of the

greatest places for students of color, particularly Latina/os, to get graduate degrees and teaching credentials. After the bad press that the College
of Education had received as a result of the dismissal of the African
American professor, the university was focused on changing its image
and marketing itself as one of the most diverse colleges in the area.

In that sense, Teresa's presence at the university was not an accident.
Her uncompromising personality did not allow her to understand to
what extent the university was using her. Teresa's presence was bringing
lots of money to the College of Education, occasionally from some grants,
but most of the time from the dozens of working-class students who were
getting into alarming student loan debt to pursue their dreams—a doctoral degree or a master's in education with a teaching credential.

Teresa taught doctoral and master's degree courses in the College of
Education. Her seminars were beyond the usual enrollment. They were
the hardest courses in the entire graduate school—very rigorous and
ideologically demanding. Caucasian students complained that they felt
attacked, and certainly, Teresa did not have any bit of political correct-
ness to accept a dissenting view. She confronted and attacked students
who publicly criticized her views. As a result, some of the students experienced ambivalent feelings of ideological dissonance and emotional conflict. Others dropped out of her courses, and some eventually developed
a strong sense of ideological clarity.

As a result, life at the College of Education was not easy for Teresa.
Her strong ideological and theoretical background, along with her deter-
rent personality, made her tenure a nightmare. Yet Laurel Canyon had to
deal with that because Teresa had an entourage of students of color who
revered her. However, there were also those who hated her. They felt
unjustly indicted by Teresa's accusatory teaching and by what they considered unfair accusations against White people. These students had the
powerful support of the conservative faculty at LCU.

Kristine, the then-director of teacher preparation, felt threatened by
Teresa, the new rising star. Teresa was younger, attractive, and theoretically powerful. Kristine astutely supported and advised Teresa's disgruntled students on how to fill her class evaluations. She had the support of these students, the power of her seniority in the college of education, and the control of teacher education to make Teresa's journey to
tenure painful. Teresa said she was aware of those dynamics.

The dean, Edward, had called Teresa many times letting her know he
was receiving anonymous letters from irritated students who complained
about the content of her classes and her "incensed" personality. However, during those years Teresa had the support of the dean of the college
and the provost of the university, who somewhat protected her from the
negative remarks that Kristine was spreading.

Teresa got tenure. Her record of publication was enough to be retained and promoted. The creation of a research institute, along with

grants and research on diversity, supported her promotion and tenure, even in the wake of several anonymous letters from students who demanded her firing.

Perhaps the fact that other faculty and students became aware of those conflicts made Teresa's teaching more popular. Students who were part of a partnership with another university drove all the way to Laurel Canyon to take her classes. Teresa's ideological and theoretical influence became inevitable. Her doctoral students were hired by the department of teacher education to become adjunct faculty, administrators, and supervisors. Two of the assistant directors of teacher education were Teresa's former doctoral students.

Gradually, Teresa's doctoral students made up 30 percent of the instructors and supervisors at the teacher education program. There was nothing Kristine could do to avoid that ideological cross-pollination. All of her strategies had failed. Progressively, Teresa's teaching on multicultural education and cultural diversity made its way into the practice and curriculum of teacher education at Laurel Canyon University. Teresa eventually was promoted to full professor.

SECTION V: VINCENT, THE TEACHER EDUCATION FACULTY

The teacher preparation program at Laurel Canyon University did not have its own tenure-line, full-time faculty. The instruction and supervision process relied mostly on doctoral students recruited from the College of Education, and their compensation did not make up for their involvement and responsibility in the success of the program. That situation exhibited the contradictory messages of the program to the preservice teachers. They were paying one of the highest tuition rates in the state, but they could not expect to be taught by tenure-line faculty in their credential courses. They only could enroll in such courses for the two electives choices of their master's degree program.

One of the faculty advisors at the teacher preparation program was Vincent, a tall, African American male, who was a former secondary teacher and was Kristine's doctoral advisee. He was one of the luminaries of the teacher education program. He brought a world of experience in urban schooling and was extraordinarily prepared to deal with the transformational nature of the teacher education program.

Vincent conducted his dissertation under Kristine's leadership, but it was Teresa who was the ideological influence behind Vincent's work. He felt torn, as he had come to Laurel Canyon University to work with Kristine in teacher education, but upon arriving there he quickly learned about the politics of race at the university and became more cautious about his alliances and about his role in the program.

Vincent became aware of how his presence in the teacher education department had been capitalized by Kristine to showcase her "multicultural" credentials. It was very late to make any changes, and he decided to do the best he could to finish his work at the department and his doctoral degree with some integrity. However, as in Teresa's situation, the university used his "colored body" to show off the program's alleged commitment to diversity.

When Samantha left the program earlier to become an assistant professor at another university, Vincent and another faculty became the co-associate directors of the teacher education department. Vincent used his position to attract, recruit, and retain students and faculty of color. He was the most popular professor among the student teachers, and one of the most rigorous. He was known for being a very conscientious individual, a tough intellectual, and a loving human being. The students adored him, and many of them considered him the most important person in the teacher preparation program.

As a doctoral student, Vincent took Teresa's courses and quickly embraced the rigorous theoretical and ideological training that she offered because it allowed him to make sense of his everyday issues with race, social class, and oppression. As a teacher education faculty and a co-associate director of the program, he used his personal experience and his theoretical awareness to create dialogical spaces and to promote critical consciousness among the student teachers. Vincent encouraged students and his own colleagues to look deeper into what was going on in teacher education.

Vincent taught the core foundation courses in the teacher preparation program, and he made everyone aware, including me, of how the program was financially benefiting from the presence of faculty and students of color. Teacher-interns were angry at how the manipulation of the "50 percent students of color" in the program could give LCU the same status as Historically Black Colleges. The students began questioning the reasons why the marketing brochures of the teacher education program were using mostly pictures of students and faculty of color.

The teacher education program became known locally and nationally by its strong emphasis on multiculturalism. The availability of some fellowship money for minority students attracted a high number of learners from underprivileged backgrounds. However, as the number of nontraditional students and minority faculty increased, tensions evolved. Under Vincent's leadership, student teachers and their faculty learned to voice their dissatisfaction with the organization of the program. The teaching of critical educational theory by Vincent and other teacher educators also contributed to that political awareness.

Students and faculty of color began questioning the multicultural credentials of the teacher education program. In classroom discussions and after class, students got together with Vincent and other faculty to reflect on the appropriation of their identity. In one of those meetings, Francisco expressed his frustration:

> In theory, education that is multicultural is a good cause. It is cause for the authentic celebration of different cultures. But I think a central point to education that is multicultural should be to strive for the elimination of inequities and injustices, but I think that it is used in this program as a novel idea that has been co-opted and has been turned into an ugly monster because it presents itself to the world as if it's doing a liberatory job when in fact, it is just a façade of the same status quo [. . .] dressed up in a nice multicultural package. In essence, teachers here are just supposed to come up multicultural superbeings.

Esther, who was part of this discussion, reflected on her presence in the program:

> See, multiculturalism is the thing they always talk about, that there are 55 percent students of color in the program. So, we're constantly reminded about how they brought us here or how they let us in, and see what a good thing they really thought. Still, doesn't seem very authentic. They're just trying to bring as many people of color here as they can, and it is not even bringing people of color, but mostly colored bodies.

Vincent's influence in this awareness process was fundamental for the changes that later evolved. He provided safe spaces and empowering experiences for students of color by creating informal support groups and by unmasking the contradictions of the department; particularly, the teacher education policy of "colored bodies."

Nancy was a newly accepted student teacher at the program. She was originally from Latin America. Her mother was a refugee in the United States, but she managed to finish college in a state university. She wanted to be a teacher, "Not only because I like kids, but because I want to be an activist and I want to be a role model for other children of immigrants like me."

Nancy remembered that one of the teacher educators who interviewed her for admission was from Spain. This interviewer was one of Kristine's mentees. She represented the distorted vision of multiculturalism that Kristine recognized: someone who spoke Spanish but was a European. Nancy said she was rejected in that interview. However, Samantha, who was the assistant director of the program at that time, reviewed all the rejections and decided to reinterview Nancy, who had enough requirements to make it into the program. Samantha accepted her and decided to become her faculty supervisor during her student teaching.

Nancy became one of the most powerful voices among the students of color. She was very dissatisfied with the program, for it did not meet her

expectations of diversity, activism, and social justice that were propagan-
dized in the marketing brochures. She finished the program eighteen
months later without really seeing any major transformation.

NOTES

1. The names of people and places mentioned in this book have been changed to
protect the identity of the participants in this research.
2. The other academic program was the master's in business administration.

FIVE

The Journey to Transform Teacher Education: Samantha's Return

SECTION I: INITIATING THE TRANSFORMATION

Samantha was brought back to direct the teacher education program at Laurel Canyon University. Kristine did not want to continue being in charge of the department. She had so many things on her mind now. Her newly encountered faith kept her busy as she traveled around the world on her quest for more religious-related experiences. Samantha became the new interim director of the department with the promise that she was going to be the internal candidate for the national search for a director of teacher education. Vincent and the other coassociate director stepped down as they both finished their doctoral degrees and were in the market looking for tenure-track jobs.

Many people in the program wondered what was the future of the teacher education program. Several of the faculty, staff, and students had experienced Kristine's hostility at work; however, they did not have any expectations about Samantha, either. There was a strong consensus that she was going to continue the same policies that Kristine had instituted. She was her mentee.

One day I bumped into Samantha when I was entering the inviting, two-level, Craftsman bungalow that housed the department of teacher education. I knew she had been appointed interim director of the program. I said hello. She greeted me and asked about my research. I told her that I had just published an article about my research on the teacher education program.

> "I criticized the multicultural approach of the teacher preparation program," I said.

She smiled at me and said, "I would love to read it."

"Great," I said.

I later thought that was going to be my opportunity to let her know what I thought about the program. I left a copy of the article in her mailbox. Days later, Samantha told me that she wanted to hear more ideas on how to move the program to a more authentic vision of multiculturalism. She wanted to address social justice issues in teacher preparation.

I was quite surprised, as I did not expect empathy from this White, middle-class teacher educator who had worked so many years under the mentorship of Kristine. That point marked the beginning of a different kind of professional relationship with her, and that conversation gave me hope that perhaps the teacher education program at Laurel Canyon could have some possibilities.

It became clear later that Samantha really wanted to move the program into a more authentic transformative direction, but she did not exactly know how to do so. She began reaching out for support, theoretically and ideologically. She was not clear how to separate herself from the legacy of manipulation and distrust that Kristine had infused into the department. She had worked under Kristine's leadership, and her arrival was announced as the return of Kristine's mentee.

In addition, Samantha wondered how her efforts could be considered legitimate and well intentioned coming from her, a White, middle-class teacher, who had taught and lived in the city of Laurel Canyon for the last ten years. It was hard for students and faculty of color to trust her. Nevertheless, Samantha assumed her role as interim director of the teacher preparation program, and during that first year she noticed how polarized and resentful the student teachers and faculty of color were. It was obvious that Kristine had been successful in crushing any possibility for real change in the department.

She decided to use her interim appointment to put the program together and to prepare herself to compete for the permanent position. She was going to take a chance. She figured she could be a new tenure-track assistant professor while running teacher education. That is what she had done in the past while writing her dissertation. She did not see any potential conflict between being a full-time administrator and a junior faculty. After all, teacher education was part of the College of Education, and she appeared to have the support and the respect of most of her former professors.

Samantha did not have an assistant director during her first year, but once she was appointed permanent director of teacher education she decided to hire one. She created a new position called assistant director for bicultural affairs, and she thought Miriam, a Latina and a graduate of the program, could understand the issues raised by bicultural teachers in the program.

Miriam was a very young teacher who, at the time of her appointment, was a second-year doctoral student working under the guidance of Teresa, the doctoral faculty. Vincent had been Miriam's supervisor when she was a student teacher in the program, and Samantha had conducted research in Miriam's classroom for her dissertation. Miriam had also taught summer school in the teacher education program and was very well known by students and the staff.

Samantha also brought back Beth, a financial wizard, who had left the department a couple of years earlier. She had worked for Kristine as the office manager of the teacher education program. However, now, with an accountant degree, Beth demanded a better position, more salary, and special time off to spend summers with her children.

Samantha felt she had to accept her conditions, as her presence was indispensable to run the program. Beth also enjoyed the support of the College of Education faculty and university administration, as she had successfully written several-million-dollar grants that had provided scholarships for students in the previous years. Beth became the assistant director for management and financial affairs.

The two newly appointed assistant directors, Miriam and Beth, were individually powerful, and together they were a commanding team. They successfully wrote several grants that funded fellowships to continue the recruitment and retention of students of color and students from nontraditional backgrounds. Financial assistance for underrepresented students was a top priority in Samantha's commitment to begin incorporating those voices into the teacher education program.

Samantha also encouraged Miriam to add more courses on bilingual education, and she invited other faculty of color to entertain ideas for new courses. She also began a deliberate effort to hire faculty and advisors who could represent the students who were admitted into the program. According to Samantha, the lack of a tenure-track system in teacher education worked at her advantage as she had the freedom to recruit her own faculty without the constraints of a more traditional faculty structure.

Samantha used that power to recruit more diverse faculty (50 percent bicultural and 38 percent bilingual) who could represent the bicultural and bilingual students who had become a relative majority in the program (66 percent) under her tenure. She also brought other educators from diverse cultural backgrounds. However, the program at Laurel Canyon was not an exception in terms of the underrepresentation of Black students and faculty.

Gradually, Samantha created more spaces for intellectual discussions, ideological growth, and shared leadership. The monthly faculty meetings became places to talk about research on teacher education. Faculty took turns presenting their research. That was an advantage of having so many doctoral students conducting research on the program. There was a

deliberate effort led by Samantha to connect the research to the pedagogical practices of the program, and more concretely, with what every single
faculty supervisor was observing in the preservice teachers' classrooms.

The faculty meetings became places for discussion and reflection on
the kind of teachers the department was seeking to prepare. Power struggles emerged as some of the faculty resisted the policies that Samantha
was instituting. The tensions and contradictions were soaring. Some of
the teacher educators were not used to thinking about teaching as a
shared, democratic practice.

Samantha insisted that faculty had to observe students' learning as a
way of assessing the teachers' competencies and dispositions. However,
some faculty wanted to continue focusing their observations on check-
lists, five-step lesson plans, rewards, and classroom management strategies. Thus, the monthly faculty meetings became dialectical spaces where
highly intellectual conversations were taking place in the midst of persistent power issues.

Most of the teacher educators were excited about attending these faculty meetings. The level of intellectual engagement and faculty participation was something new in the department. Every aspect and phase of
the teacher preparation program was deeply scrutinized and evaluated.

Samantha used the research on teacher education and her years of
exemplary teaching to instill the teacher preparation at Laurel Canyon
with sound pedagogical practices and a clear vision of the purpose of
public education. Samantha had definitely opened up the doors for a
shared leadership and faculty, and students gradually felt empowered to
bring up issues and to discuss them individually with her or in public
meetings.

That was the case one afternoon in the spring semester when a famous
teacher educator was invited to address the entire cohort of preservice
teachers. There were more than one hundred teachers seated in the big
auditorium of the College of Education. It was an intimidating place. It
was dark and concave; however, the chairs were very comfortable. The
stadiumlike seating arrangement and the lights made it difficult for the
speakers to establish eye contact with the audience.

That evening was one of those teaching sessions when all the preservice and in-service teachers were required to attend a special lecture on
urban education. There was anticipation and eagerness to hear the guest
speaker. Nothing seemed more appropriate than to bring a veteran revolutionary educator from the East Coast to address the concerns of this
cohort who had been formed into the principles of critical educational
theory.

Because the students had had an intense experience voicing their
opinions and had been socialized in the program to defend their positions and experiences, they began making comments and asking questions very early in the lecture. They engaged aggressively in a dialogue

with the guest speaker, particularly when he refused to address issues of race and gender in his presentation.

The guest speaker was shocked by the confronting attitude of the students, and he reacted rudely when he felt these young, novice teachers questioned his revolutionary credentials. The teachers felt that his views about educating inner-city children were not accurate, for they had not included an examination of racism and sexism in the classroom and in teacher preparation.

What was supposed to be an important lecture on teaching disadvantaged students became a verbal battlefield. The teachers publicly confronted and recriminated each other in the presence of the guest lecturer while the attending faculty took sides with those who represented their views. The speaker abruptly left the auditorium, and the students followed.

The next day, a group of teacher educators demanded an urgent faculty meeting. They urged Samantha to review and reconsider the philosophy of the program. Samantha, with the support of some of the faculty, bravely defended the right of the students to question a situation where they felt excluded. However, a significant number of supervisors and adjunct faculty felt that the discomfort expressed by the students did not meet the expectations of a graduate school. They expressed disappointment about Samantha's decision to not reprimand the teachers.

It was clear that Samantha was siding with the students. That was a turning point in the development of the program. Samantha had finally established her leadership. She continued being affable and friendly, but it was clear that ideologically she had begun to change. She did not side with her more disgruntled, conservative faculty—the larger group of White, middle-class, former teachers and administrators—who refused to change their beliefs about teaching preparation.

SECTION II: PATRICK, THE MATH FACULTY

Samantha knew that one of the flaws of the program was the lack of faculty expertise to support the interns who were obtaining single-subject credentials. Second-language acquisition, math, and science were the weakest areas of the program. Thus, she decided to hire Patrick, a Caucasian, veteran educator, as an adjunct faculty and teacher supervisor to devote more time to the preparation and support of aspiring math and science teachers. Samantha was aware that Kristine had recruited Patrick a couple of years ago to teach summer school and she had encouraged him to pursue his doctoral degree, and, she said, she thought he was a very ethical educator.

Patrick's arrival coincided with the gradual changes Samantha was implementing in the teacher preparation program. His jovial attitude and humble manners were an asset in his relationship with students and faculty. In spite of the hard questions he always asked, no one ever felt intimidated by him. He was one of the few teacher educators who began looking at students' learning to track teachers' performance in a time when no one had ever heard about that concept. As Samantha recalled later, his influence in the development of the program was undeniable:

> Patrick put a lot of teachers on the line because they were not looking at the students' learning. He asked difficult questions in the faculty meetings. How do you know what your preservice teachers are doing? You need to look at their students' learning. We did not have any idea whether our preservice and in-service teachers were influencing the learning of their students.

Patrick's mantra about student learning became the focus of many faculty meetings, and he helped Samantha and the rest of the faculty to understand the complexities of teacher supervision, classroom observation, and teachers' performance. Several times he presented to the rest of faculty the artifacts that demonstrated his in-service teachers' growth. They were the work that the students had completed in the classrooms where his teachers taught. That included students' homework, math projects, and special assignments rather than test scores.

However, Patrick did not limit himself to his area of expertise. He greatly contributed to the success of bilingual teachers. He helped rewrite the classroom observation protocol to supervise in-service teachers, and he avidly shared the intense, and at times traumatic, internship experience of the student teachers. He brought to the faculty meetings teachers' journals to raise attention about the need to improve the teacher preparation process and to adequately support teacher candidates.

Patrick worked with Samantha to obtain two major grants to increase the recruitment of math teachers and to extend the duration of their practicum so that they would have time to become more reflective and knowledgeable. Patrick's cadre of mathematic teachers was impressive. With funding from the grant he had obtained earlier, he held several institutes where the math teachers debriefed their learning and teaching experiences and prepared to present papers at major research conferences. In reflecting about his students, Patrick said:

> I just got an email yesterday from one of our past teacher interns, [Jose]. Do you remember [him]? He's now an assistant professor in math education at [Longview] University. His research focus is on sociocultural curriculum in math education at the secondary level. He gives the [Laurel Canyon] program a great deal of credit for his advancement. He found me on the Internet; I just had presented at a state math conference in [Texas] where I exhibited and discussed my community college student's math portfolios and how I used them to develop alternative assessments in math education.

Patrick's level of intellectual curiosity, candor, and acute understanding of the process of learning to teach was the major catalyst in the process of transforming teacher preparation. Patrick's joy and intellectual excitement kept Samantha, and the entire faculty at the department, intensely engaged and hopeful about the future of teacher education.

SECTION III: THE PHILOSOPHY OF THE TEACHER EDUCATION PROGRAM

Early in the development of the teacher education program, Kristine was the one that infused the teacher preparation program at Laurel Canyon University with a constructivist theory of learning. That was a very revolutionary approach at that time. The entire teacher preparation program was developed based on Piaget pedagogical principles, and the students got a clear sense of the theoretical foundation of the program since the moment they took the first course and read *The Constructivist Classroom, Teaching Children to Care*, and *Building a Community of Learners*.

Samantha had inherited the program with its constructivist philosophy where student teachers learned firsthand the concept of *learning by doing* through their short but intense student-teaching experiences. Since early in the program, students knew that the Laurel Canyon Teacher Preparation Program expected them to become constructivist teachers. The students felt that it was common sense how constructivism explained teaching and learning.

However, they were shocked beyond explanation once they were thrown in a classroom for the intensive internship experience. The student teachers realized there was no way they could become constructivist teachers considering the contradictions they were witnessing in the classroom and the conservative policies of the schools. That constant shock was articulated in their weekly journals that were shared with their faculty supervisors, who at the same time brought up these concerns in the monthly faculty meetings.

During those discussions, the teacher education faculty focused on how to help the candidates not only to acquire the knowledge and skills to become excellent teachers but also how to strategize and do their work without giving up their ideals so they would not quit teaching. The process of teacher preparation at Laurel Canyon under Samantha's leadership was permanently dialogical, reflective, research oriented, and pragmatic. No one was alone. Faculty depended on each other to help the in-service teachers understand the contradictions of school life, and students relied on their peers and their faculty supervisors to get through the week.

Since Samantha arrived at the program, there were some occasional talks on socioconstructivism, but Lev Vygotsky was never officially part of the teacher preparation experience. Samantha alluded to the Zones of Proximal Development when teaching reading to the in-service teachers. However, looking retrospectively, the formal integration of socioconstructivism would have helped the program to solidify and prepare teachers more effectively. Nonetheless, when I interviewed teachers who graduated from the program, they told me that it was the constructivist philosophy of teaching that had drawn them into this teacher preparation:

> I believe that the philosophy of education at Laurel Canyon Teacher Education Program is an excellent concept. We learned by doing. That is what drew me to the program.

> I think the critical aspect of the teacher preparation philosophy is invaluable, that if anything, more time could be spent incorporating or at least discussing the theoretical and practical implications of its philosophy.

> It is student-centered. It modeled effective method for us. Self-reflection and meta-cognition are important at all levels of learning. It also helped me realize that my philosophy [of teaching] is ever evolving.

However, it was obvious that there had been some changes to that constructivist philosophy of the teacher preparation program since Samantha began directing the program. She gradually infused the department with a more critical stance: an antibias, antiracist pedagogy. The strong influence of a cadre of doctoral students grounded in critical pedagogy was influential in this vision. They were now an intrinsic part of the teacher preparation program.

After years of propagandizing the multicultural nature of the teacher education program, Samantha had gradually realized that the program under Kristine's leadership had co-opted these revolutionary credentials. She was ready to move the department beyond the policy of "colored bodies." She made changes to the introductory course of the program to infuse its content with a critical vision of education in the tradition of critical pedagogy. She made sure that this initial course provided student teachers with the background and support to open their minds for what they were going to experience through their process of becoming teachers.

The continued discussion about the philosophy of the program in faculty meetings and other forums had led to the official recognition that education was eminently political, and as such, education was implicated in the reproduction of detrimental teaching practices for culturally diverse students.

There was a big emphasis in the teacher preparation on discussing meritocracy, tracking, ability grouping, standardized testing, teacher expectations, and the hidden curriculum. Samantha openly stated her expectation that the mission of teachers was to form critical citizens and reclaim the real meaning of democracy and social justice in the tradition of John Dewey and Maxine Greene.

I decided to gather data from the entire cohort of teacher interns to find out how they were visualizing these changes. I wanted to explore whether the program's concerns for social justice were important to them. This is how they verbalized their views:

> I think social justice should be among our top three concerns if not underlying our very reason for teaching. I realize that some [teachers] don't look at teaching as a political act, but I feel I'd be denying myself if I try to divorce my career from my beliefs.

> Hell, Yes! I mean absolutely! And it should not be a discussion. It needs to be an in-depth examination of culture and society and cause teachers to be introspective about their own biases and beliefs.

> I think teachers should definitely be concerned with issues of social justice in the classroom because we are in a position to teach and model about life. That includes more than just reading, writing, and arithmetic. It is about preparing our children to be responsible and caring citizens of the future [. . .] teachers must take on this role for the community.

After that day I became convinced that something was under way that was changing the in-service teachers' beliefs about teaching and social justice. Samantha's commitment to forming teachers who could be advocates and to develop a passion for learning and reading in all their students was beginning to evolve. That was just during her second year of tenure.

SECTION IV: THE CURRICULUM AND THE METHOD COURSES AT LAUREL CANYON TEACHER PREPARATION

When Samantha became the permanent director of the teacher education department, she decided to eliminate the only two existing courses on multicultural education, as it was evident that they portrayed the vision of an add-on approach to diversity. She revised the entire teacher education curriculum and made sure all courses were infused with a critical view about schooling that was inclusive of all forms of cultural differences.

Samantha also paid special attention to the literacy curriculum because that was her area of expertise. She reviewed the readings courses and met regularly with all the instructors to evaluate the content of the lessons and their pedagogical approaches. The concept of critical literacy, authentic assessment, and students' prior literacy experiences became central to this discussion. For the first time the literacy instructors began planning the courses as a team. Led by Samantha, the faculty chose the books, the literacy activities, and, more importantly, the program approach to reading, as described in the following planning meeting:

> Now what about the portfolio? Are there specific things that should be in the portfolio that we should write out so that they know or do you wanna [*sic*] leave it open? What are the things they have to do?

> They have to do a literacy autobiography, is that ok with everybody?

> *Yes.*

> That's where they write about their own experiences of reading and writing. They are doing the [language] assessment, should that be in their portfolio? Would that be useful to be in there?

> They are going to learn from it, they are going at the end to have a whole reflection of what's the big picture here. So, they should have a final definition of literacy. So that would be point number two, develop a definition of literacy, right. Their learning log is just for them . . . they could find excerpts that they wanted to include; they could use the learning log and their personal experiences to illustrate things that they want . . . if they want to illustrate something more. What about the planning? What kind of plans do you want them to have?

> I think they should have phonemic awareness, as well as, depending on what grade level they have how are they going to . . . well they can plan it they just wouldn't be able to teach it if they have upper grades. So all they have to do is plan it, they don't have to teach it?

> I think, I think that maybe because you do that more in the lower grades, but I think everyone should just do like it could be a vocabulary assignment, a spelling assignment, I mean they could do at whatever level.

> I put here, umm, the student will demonstrate knowledge of and ability to apply appropriate strategies for developing children's phonemic awareness, phonics, knowledge, spelling, and language arts. They have a choice, they just have to plan and teach a lesson, now during a semester course I have them do each one, but maybe for the summer they could just pick two areas.

> What were the ones you listed?

> Phonemic awareness, phonics, knowledge, spelling and language arts. It could be vocabulary development also. So the whole year they do all four, they have all semester.

Under Kristine's administration, literacy had been regarded by some graduates of the program as one of the neglected areas in the teacher preparation process. However, under Samantha's leadership, literacy became a strong bastion of the program. It became an intrinsic part of the philosophy of teacher preparation.

When I had asked the interns about whether the teacher education program at Laurel Canyon was addressing issues of social justice, they immediately recalled one of their literacy textbooks that Samantha had included in the reading courses.

> I think the program addresses the issue of social justice for the most part, especially after reading the book *Literacies of Power* by Macedo that addresses the issue of critical pedagogy and how we as teachers should make it known to children.

> Of course teachers should be concerned with social justice. Macedo wrote about teaching children to "read the world." That is, to become aware of social injustices and contradictions between what the United States purports itself to be and what is really is.

> I believe [Laurel Canyon] addressed the issues of social justice. Macedo's book was an eye-opening experience for my fellow classmates and me.

One of the many innovations implemented in the literacy classes was the integration of the Learning Record as the official method of assessment of the program and as an alternative to the obsession with standardized testing. Samantha clearly articulated how authentic assessment was the key to good teaching. She argued that authentic assessment, particularly the Learning Record, placed students in control of their own learning because they were made aware of the benchmarks and what they have to accomplish in order to move to the next grade level.

Authentic assessment became the top priority of Samantha. She devoted most of her time to infuse the education of teachers at Laurel Canyon with the belief that is possible to assess children holistically and to comply with state standards. In-service teachers learned how to use miscue analysis, running records, literacy portfolios, and to develop rubrics to track their students' learning.

There was also a strong emphasis on using literature circles, modeling guided reading, teaching the writing process, and using poetry dialogues. The literacy faculty led by Samantha emphasized the use of multicultural children's books, social justice literature, and children's books written in a foreign language, particularly Spanish. Fortunately, the teacher education program had been able to put together one of the best children's libraries in town, and teachers had at their disposal the latest children's literature for use in their classrooms.

Samantha also made sure the interns were able to connect the significance of authentic assessment with teachers' understanding of their students and their families. The in-service teachers had to complete literacy profiles of some of their own students as part of the assignments for the reading classes. That assessment included interviews of students, parents, home visits, and neighborhood maps.

The success of this cutting-edge assessment tool encouraged many schools and districts to develop a partnership with the Laurel Canyon teacher preparation program. The efforts to integrate critical literacy with the teaching of the Learning Record while asking the interns to write their own literacy biographies became a central piece in helping in-service teachers see the big picture of schooling.

The credential analyst of the teacher education department confirmed that about 96 percent of the in-service teachers had passed the state reading test—just two years after Samantha took the leadership of the program. That percentage was in complete opposition to what was happening in other larger teacher preparation programs in California.

With the assistance of Miriam, the assistant director for bicultural affairs, and Francisco, one of the bilingual faculty, the teacher preparation department began offering a new literacy class on second-language acquisition and a culture and reading class in Spanish to support bilingual teachers. Samantha also incorporated two major workshops on gay and lesbian issues, which were led by gay district personnel and principals. It was essential that interns could identify with issues of sexual orientation based on the experiences of their fellow educators.

SECTION V: TEACHING PRACTICES

One of Samantha's most important challenges to the philosophy of the program was to move the discourse of multiculturalism from a celebration of heroes, food, and festivals to an examination of the impact of detrimental teaching practices on culturally diverse students. Samantha used every faculty meeting and team-teaching planning session to question these practices and to provide alternative pedagogical strategies. However, it was clear that faculty struggled with these principles, which in most of the cases contradicted their own teaching experience.

Classroom environment was the topic of one of the first and last courses of the internship experience. Interns were strongly encouraged to question the reward and punishment strategies that were so pervasive in the K–12 system. They were urged to critique and reflect on the pros and cons of detention and times out, the dehumanizing aspects of writing standards, and the bribe system that saturated most disciplinary models at schools.

Interns and instructors engaged in intense dialogues about the consequences of tracking and grouping by ability level. They learned about the significance of motivation, creation of community circles, and the inclusion of students' experiences in the classroom as fundamental to avoid disciplinary problems. The program emphasized the notion that students were the very reason to teach, and therefore, teachers should develop strategies to assure their success.

In the introductory course of the program, teachers became familiar-ized with the politics of textbook adoption, official knowledge, hidden curriculum, subjugated knowledge of their students, and the multiple stakeholders of teacher education. This knowledge continued to be em-phasized throughout the entire program. Math and science faculty who were also exemplary classroom teachers questioned the assumed neutral-ity of these hard subjects and helped interns examine how they could differentiate their instruction even when they taught biology, algebra, calculus, or physics.

The faculty led by Samantha demanded rigorous planning from their interns. They were convinced that lesson planning was the most essential tool to become an excellent teacher. However, Samantha and the faculty were not talking about the typical lesson plans. They encouraged teach-ers to reflect on the values and assumption they had, as they were engag-ing in planning. The teachers were told that their lessons should include essential questions, a do section, a reflection question, and the assessment that needed to happen before and after the lesson. It was a cyclical pro-cess.

The message to the teachers was clear: progressive ideologies were not enough to be a successful educator. The program expected teachers to teach an antibiased, antiracist, rigorous curriculum, but it also demanded rigorous planning, constant reflection, and excellent teaching. In Saman-tha's view, effective teaching practices were an integral element of social justice advocacy.

SECTION VI: TEACHERS AS REFLECTIVE RESEARCHERS

The capstone experience of the program was the completion of an action research project conducted by the teachers in their classroom and the community in which they taught. Initially this assignment was criticized because it did not conform to the traditional requirements of a master's thesis. However, Vincent, the African American faculty, changed the original version and added a theoretical framework, a literature review section, and infused this final assignment with more rigorous methodo-logical standards.

During the final semester of the program, the coursework was de-signed to support the completion of the action research project, and therefore, the courses addressed issues of community, diversity, and crit-ical educational theory. Teachers were asked to examine their upbringing and analyze how that experience shaped their ideologies. Because they were asked to write their literacy autobiographies during the semester, they understood how their life histories shaped their philosophy of teach-ing. It was at this stage of completing the capstone experience when teachers began to really problematize their views and experiences about teaching assisted by the literature.

Teachers also learned about different research methodologies including action research, ethnography, narrative, and interview studies. They became familiar with different methods of data collection to investigate the lives of their students and their parents. For an entire semester the teachers observed, took field notes, interviewed, and understood the world of their students. At the end, it was obvious that their inquiry projects had become a transformative experience.

The action research assignment made them realize that the university had initiated the process of teacher preparation, but the teachers had taken ownership of this learning process in the interaction they had developed with the students and their families. They began to connect with the community where they taught and to understood that this relationship was fundamental to anchor their teaching.

As Ramiro, one of the teachers at Cabrillo Elementary School and a graduate of the teacher education program, said,

> Had I not had the experience at [Laurel Canyon], I would not have had the opportunity of connecting the dots. It's a matter of disposition. You had a goal, a political endeavor. I cannot divorce both. I have become a better teacher—experienced, skilled, [with knowledge of] strategies, and methodology, process of reflection, self-awareness. [The program] gave me a space for dialogue, discussion, [I learned] what is to be critical, what is pedagogy.

SIX

What Went Wrong? The Accountability Movement Arrived at the College of Education

There was a tenuous feeling of hope and excitement in the air. Some faculty and students began asking themselves, "Is all this talk about transforming teacher education real?" During Teresa's seminar, students constantly asked her, "How can we bring to life the principles of critical pedagogy? How can we implement these principles in our lives in our classrooms?" It appeared that in this teacher education program, students and faculty were beginning to identify the specific actions and strategies embedded in a critical cultural politics that would make teacher preparation a compelling, transformative experience.

Samantha began putting into practice her notion of what a critical teacher preparation program should be. She visualized teachers as advocates, but she believed they needed to be first solid, excellent educators. By demystifying everything, from classroom environment to teaching to read the world, she conveyed to the teachers that the heart of teaching was about instilling an intense joy and passion for learning. It was about using literacy to develop students' voices.

However, simultaneously to that critical commitment, some contradictions were taking place in the department of teacher education. There was a growing conflict in the administration of the program that involved the staff and the assistant directors. The conflict had become unmanageable, and unfortunately, for everyone involved, the struggle had evolved along race lines.

SECTION I: THE TWO ASSISTANT DIRECTORS — THE POLITICS OF RACE

The animosity between Beth and Miriam, the assistant directors of the teacher preparation program at Laurel Canyon, grew ostensibly. Samantha, who was conscious of her Whiteness, expressed that she wanted to move away from the policy of colored bodies that had characterized Kristine's legacy. She was committed to give effective power and voice to the newly hired staff and faculty of color. She could have hired a single assistant director as Kristine had done in the past. However, she recognized the significance of creating a top administrative position for bicultural affairs.

At the same time, Samantha also agreed with the university that the return of Beth, the former office manager under Kristine, was indispensable for the continued financial success of the program. Samantha agreed with all the conditions Beth demanded for her return, including a new title and extraordinary perks. At the end, Samantha ended up with two assistant directors with allegedly two different job descriptions, but with clearly overlapping functions that created additional frictions.

Samantha's easygoing personality clearly contrasted with the iron-hand leadership of Kristine. She made everyone around her feel comfortable rather than intimidated. Thus, Miriam, the assistant director for bicultural affairs, throve in that environment. As an eloquent activist and veteran educator, Miriam had become a role model for the young, Latino/a teachers as well as for the growing Latino staff that looked at her as their leader.

Thus, the loyalties and affinities were divided in the teacher education department along race lines. The young, Latino, entry-level staff hummed around Miriam and the teachers of color. The more middle-age, Caucasian personnel expressed their allegiances to Beth, who was the office manager and who ran all the administrative and financial affairs of the department.

Beth had worked under Kristine's leadership for so many years that she was the most senior person among the faculty and staff at the program. Her personality, physical stature, and seniority gave her an absolute sense of authority and control over the business of teacher preparation. In spite of the fact that Miriam's position was more academic and Beth's position was administrative, they found themselves clashing with each other on issues that had to be resolved at both levels.

Beth enjoyed the confidence of the university and college administrators. From their viewpoint, Beth was the only one who signified the *business as usual* approach in the ever-changing department of teacher education under Samantha's new leadership. Beth made sure that the dean of the College of Education, the staff of the new provost, and the staff of the president of the university were informed about everything that was going on in teacher education. Even Samantha did not have the same level of access and confidence that Beth enjoyed in the highest tiers of the university administration.

On the other hand, Miriam's assertive and eloquent personality was an asset in her relationship with the senior faculty and administrators of the university. Faculty and staff at the teacher education department were pleased with her presence at Laurel Canyon. The pretty, educated young woman looked easygoing and comfortable navigating the intricate academic and administrative world of the university.

The disagreements between Beth and Miriam increased at the end of their first year. When summer approached, Miriam remembered that Beth had negotiated six weeks of vacation to spend with her kids during summertime. Miriam considered that extraordinary benefit not only unjust but also administratively disastrous, as summer was the beginning of the academic year for the new student teachers.

Miriam thought that Beth was given this special privilege because of her seniority and skin color. Miriam also said that Beth was making more money than her, in spite of the fact that both of them had the same rank of assistant director at the teacher preparation program.

Samantha said that was not true. "They both made the same amount." Samantha alleged that Miriam's salary was at the top of her rank in the university. Samantha said that to compensate for the extra vacations she gave to Beth she allowed Miriam to teach up to four classes during her work hours, including summer, which would add $20,000 more per year to Miriam's salary.

> I thought I'd balance the vacation with [Miriam's] teaching salary. Her classes were mostly within her working hours, so she actually got extra pay.

Thus, tired of complaining about what she thought was unfair treatment, Miriam devoted her summers to teach summer school to the new student teachers. The downside of that decision was that she did not have time to take care of her administrative responsibilities at the teacher preparation program. Hence, by virtue of this kind of employment negotiation, Samantha ended up having no assistant director during summer school (just Miriam part time), making her professional life, as the director of teacher preparation, a complete ordeal.

Samantha's already unmanageable schedule was out of control, and consequently, her stress level. Samantha did what she always did in those kinds of situations: she completed the more urgent work that needed to be finished, she neglected other projects, took on more responsibilities in the department, wrote grants, taught classes, led and planned seminars, advised students, counseled faculty, confronted disgruntled administrators, and took little care of her publications, her health, and personal life.

By the fall semester Samantha was able to get a substantive raise for Miriam.

"She was making almost as much as an assistant professor and almost the same as the senior director of the doctoral center." Nevertheless, Samantha was becoming tired of what she perceived as Miriam's lack of responsibility. Samantha told me that she had that perception of her even before the salary crisis had emerged, as Miriam began collaborating full time in a community-based project away from her responsibilities at teacher education.

Samantha thought she had provided so much support for Miriam and in return she got this person who appeared to be very immature and did not care about teacher education. Miriam was absent for long periods of time. She was immersed in other political projects that kept her from actively participating in the daily life of the department. Between her doctoral program, her community-based activism, and her summer teaching, Miriam had very little time left to contribute to the growth of the teacher preparation program. So Samantha decided to confront Miriam on her poor professional performance.

> "She's gone much of the time and she's angry when I bring up this issue," said Samantha.

During the faculty meetings and faculty retreats Miriam was always absent, and when physically present, she did not participate in the discussions. She told Samantha, "I don't want to do this all my life."

Miriam looked unhappy and unrealized. Even her teaching was not as inspiring and exciting as before.

News of the clash and disappointments with Miriam spread across the College of Education. Miriam used her political power and intellectual authority to make sure that everybody in the college and the university administration knew that she felt harassed by Samantha and Beth. Teresa was the chair of Miriam's doctoral dissertation committee, and she became furious at Samantha for what she considered unfair treatment of Miriam and preferential consideration to Beth.

Samantha said that the irony of the situation began to unfold in the fourth summer after Miriam's appointment. She said she had created a new position for Miriam to give voice and leadership to faculty and students of color, and now Miriam was denouncing her and Beth for racial harassment and unfair treatment. Samantha said she did not know how racialized the relationships in the department had evolved, and she had no idea how to handle them, particularly at the administrative level.

Samantha did not know, but the administration of the university and the College of Education were carefully watching her actions. They were assessing the impact of these conflicts and Samantha's policies on the viability of the teacher education program. The administration could not afford to jeopardize its more profitable department.

SECTION II: THE REALIGNMENT OF THE CONSERVATIVE FORCES TO TAKE CONTROL OF TEACHER EDUCATION

Meanwhile, the balancing forces of the College of Education had shifted considerably in the last few years. While Teresa was on sabbatical, a new Asian American faculty male was recruited. Glen, who had been the school superintendent of a major school district, was hired as an assistant professor at the College of Education. However, it became clear after the first year that Glen did not want to publish, so he resigned the tenure-track position and was offered a full-time, term-faculty appointment.

Samantha remembered meeting Glen several years earlier when she approached a number of school districts to place new student teachers. "He was a very arrogant administrator," she remembered. Samantha also learned that he had a bad reputation among the teachers in his district. However, at the LCU's College of Education, Glen was well liked by everyone, but particularly by his male colleagues. As the only practitioner male of color in the faculty body, he became a powerful force in the College of Education.

Glen's arrival coincided with one of the most pivotal moments in educational history in the United States: the consolidation of the standardization and testing movement. This was something Glen was very good at. Tests and standards were his area of expertise as the superintendent of the school district where he used to work, and this was the strong background he was bringing to Laurel Canyon University.

Many things were problematic at the College of Education, but there was one situation that was tacitly accepted: the autonomy of the teacher education department. Under Kristine's strong control, no one in the College of Education would intervene in the business of preparing school-teachers unless Kristine invited them. However, since Samantha took the direction of teacher education, things were different. From time to time, the dean, some professors, or college administrators dropped by unannounced by the department whenever there were events that involved important decisions regarding the preparation of teachers.

This was particularly more noticeable since the enrollment at teacher education had been declining. However, the diminishing enrollment was not a new situation or a sign of something going wrong. According to Samantha, teacher education always had a regular cycle of ups and downs over the years. In one of the faculty meetings, she acknowledged the difficult financial situation:

> First of all, our budget . . . we're really budgeted. We're really in trouble. The whole university is in trouble actually. So, 'cause [*sic*] we only have eighty-four students and our Xerox budget is always huge. If you have like real neat packets of something and the [teachers] want to borrow, you can make one packet if you don't want to lose yours. You

know, make just one copy that could be passed around in class, that
they can copy from it if they want.

Edward, the dean, was concerned about what was going on in teacher
education and asked Glen to help with the department. In fact, initially
Glen had been offered the position of director of teacher education, but
he had declined it because he did not consider it worthy. However, after
a few years it appeared he had second thoughts. The dean thought Glen's
former superintendent experience would be well used in that area.

The dean barely informed Samantha about the decision to have Glen
help her when she noticed that Glen was already intruding into the department and questioning the philosophy of the teacher preparation program. Glen began teaching the master's degree classes for teachers, and
some of them began complaining not only about his poor teaching but
also about the contradictory messages they were receiving from him.
According to some of the students, his courses focused entirely on the
fundamental role of test scores and classroom management skills to be a
good teacher.

Some faculty supervisors were upset at Glen as he kept undermining
the intensive work they had done with the teachers to introduce them to
a more progressive vision of teaching. They were dismayed at how condescendingly he was talking about Samantha and about the quality of the
teacher preparation program.

Glen was particularly annoyed at the final Action Research Project
that the teachers conducted with their students as the capstone experience of their teacher preparation program. He and Larry, the educational
policy expert, began dropping by unannounced at the core seminars of
the teacher education program and the most important public lectures to
confirm their suspicions that the students were not learning what they
considered to be the indispensable knowledge to become good teachers.

Glen insisted that the teachers that Laurel Canyon was preparing did
not meet the demands of urban schools. In meetings with some of his
colleagues, doctoral students, and teachers, he expressed his concerns
that the teacher preparation program was disorganized, the student
teachers had too much power, and the curriculum was saturated with
students' needs and prior experiences. He said that he believed the program was not doing a good job of forming teachers.

Glen argued that instead of learning about authentic assessment, bilingual education, and critical literacy, teachers should have been learning about standards, strong management skills, test scores, and scripted
curriculum. He argued that school administrators like him would not
hire the kind of teachers Samantha was forming.

Glen was successful at persuading faculty at the College of Education
about the imminent collapse of the teacher preparation program if the
university did not intervene. After all, he had been a school administrator

all his life, and the faculty thought that there was nobody better than him, a former superintendent, to evaluate the kind of teaching and learning that Samantha had implemented in teacher preparation.

It was in the midst of these developments that the issues with Miriam, the assistant director for bicultural affairs, arose. All the eyes of the faculty and administrators became focused on teacher education. Was Samantha strong enough to keep the program robust and working? What kinds of teachers was the program preparing? What was all that talk about authentic assessment? Could Samantha keep her act together instead of falling prey to all her talk about bilingualism, multiculturalism, and anti-bias pedagogy? Was the declining enrollment at teacher education a sign that the program was failing?

SECTION III: PREPARING ADMINISTRATORS AND TEACHERS TO WORK IN AN ERA OF ACCOUNTABILITY

The College of Education was so eager to give Glen a professional space at Laurel Canyon's College of Education that most of his colleagues were thrilled when they heard his plans to create a new doctoral program to train school superintendents like him. Glen had become a close friend of Larry, an educational policy expert.

In a few months, with the support of the dean and the university, Glen and Larry launched a new intensive PhD program in Urban Leadership. They recruited students from their district networks and offered generous fellowships, in addition to the promise of a high-quality, intensive doctorate in one of the most prestigious universities in the area that could land students a school superintendent job.

The PhD program hardly made it through the first years. It was losing money, and it also became clear that the other PhD programs in education were not doing well either. They could not sustain themselves only with the small tuition they were bringing to the university. This is why there were growing concerns about the drastic drop in enrollment in teacher education.

The administration of the college and the university knew that teacher education was the only department in the entire College of Education that was making abundant money to subsidize the other doctorates. Thus, teacher education became more pressured not only to increase student enrollment but also to prepare the kinds of teachers that could please the administrators that Glen and Larry were preparing to lead the school districts in the area.

Faculty in the college of education were invited to teach the selected group of school administrators who once a week came to Laurel Canyon to take classes. One day Samantha was invited by Glen to teach the small cohort, and she decided to focus her talk on the advantages of authentic assessment, particularly, the Learning Record, to improve academic achievement.

Samantha used as an example Cabrillo Elementary School from a neighbor district whose students were mostly working-class, Latino children. She showed how the school was steadily moving from being one of the lowest-achieving schools to becoming a higher-achieving school with bilingual students because of the adoption of authentic performance assessment, although, Samantha said that "the test scores were still low, partly because the students were still learning English and the tests were administered in English."

Samantha said that the response from the administrators in Glen's class was cold and hostile. They could not see how such an intensive and complex assessment could replace the standardized tests that had become mandatory in the last few years. The incredulity and disappointment was obvious in this group of doctoral students. Samantha said there were attacks and then, hostile silence. She left very sad and angry. She felt her colleague Glen had set her up.

SECTION IV: BREAKING DOWN SAMANTHA'S SUPPORT SYSTEM: THE DISMANTLING OF CABRILLO ELEMENTARY SCHOOL

Glen and Larry began an intensive campaign to discredit Samantha and the philosophy of the teacher preparation program. They mounted an aggressive offensive to dismantle her support system in the schools and districts where she had acquired significant influence. One of those initiatives focused on Cabrillo Elementary School in the neighbor city of Cabrillo.

Many of the teachers at that school were graduates of the Laurel Canyon Teacher Education Program. They had been Samantha's students, and now they were her colleagues. The entire school, with the district support, had become one of the leading schools to implement the Learning Record as the primary method of assessment. Test scores were used to provide the official data to the city and the state, but the Learning Record was used to assess students' academic achievement and to inform instruction in both English and Spanish.

The challenges had been steep. Most of the student population was on free or reduced lunch, and about 75 percent of the students were second-language learners. One of the bilingual teachers, who was a graduate of the program at Laurel Canyon, said,

> In the three years I was there, I was able to see patterns of academic achievement by the students. They became critical thinkers. I could see Bloom's taxonomy . . . bilingual, biliterate . . . when they had those [first] three years, kindergarten, first grade, second grade, and third grade they became problem solvers.

In a few years, the schoolteachers became leaders and moderators of the Learning Record, and they were able to train other teachers on how to use this authentic assessment in their schools. During one of the semesters, Laurel Canyon University served as the site for a conference where Native American teachers from across the nation came for further preparation and training to implement the Learning Record in their reservations. The teachers' leaders from Cabrillo Elementary School were the panelists and moderators of the workshops.

Cabrillo Elementary School had unintentionally become a professional development school. When the antibilingual legislation was approved in California, the teachers and the principal of the school advised the bilingual parents to sign bilingual wavers that allowed the school to remain fully bilingual even in the midst of the most aggressive antibilingual campaigns. When the state ordered administrators and teachers to administer a norm-reference achievement test to every single child, Cabrillo Elementary School was able to obtain waivers from the parents, as its student population was mostly English-language learners.

The school continued with authentic assessment activities while actively collaborating with the teacher preparation program at Laurel Canyon. Several students conducted their student teaching at Cabrillo Elementary, and senior teachers from the school taught method courses at the university. It was a true professional development partnership and one of the greatest successes in the area.

Meanwhile, Glen and Larry were able to write several grants and obtain consulting jobs in several districts in the area, including Cabrillo School District. They also began offering free professional development at several schools, including Cabrillo Elementary. In a matter of a few months, Glen and Larry had convinced the superintendent of Cabrillo School District that the Learning Record was in total contradiction with the newer state and federal policies that demanded standardized testing and teaching to the test. Glen and Larry were able to demonstrate how much time the school and staff were wasting by implementing that kind of assessment.

By the end of the academic year, the Learning Record had been eliminated from Cabrillo Elementary School. The principal was transferred to a maintenance position in the district, and the tenured teachers were transferred to other schools. As one of the former teachers said,

> By [the end of the year] they had removed our principal. So, what happened with him was that he supported us. He was a moderator for the Learning Record. His philosophy in terms of leadership was collaborative, and he was a consummate leader where he would be very adamant about [forming] strong, armed teachers who weren't pulling weight. But at the same time too, his pedagogy was informed by multiage classrooms, by inclusion. So, he was way above and beyond what most leaders at the time . . . and people were considering how or what

inclusion meant in their schools he was doing it, and doing language programs and parent involvement, and it was an interesting environment. They had to get rid of him first. They had to remove him first, and they offered him an early retirement, he wouldn't take it. They offered him a higher leadership position where he would be able to direct us in that general area, he wouldn't take it.

A new principal was hired, and according to one of the teachers, "His job was to dismantle the Learning Record. There was a witch hunt against [Laurel Canyon] teachers and the Learning Record people."

The new administration filed a grievance against the teacher leader of the school, Mannie. He was very loved by the teacher candidates at Laurel Canyon, as he taught every year several courses on bilingual education and authentic assessment in English and Spanish. The new principal asked Mannie to leave the classroom in the middle of the school year. As one of his colleagues recalls:

> He was a master teacher; he had tenure. Not only that, he actually mentored a lot of people, not just there. Many in [Cabrillo] Unified, many in the surrounding school districts. He was a professor at the university. I think they had no other recourse [. . .] they had an open investigation on him. They wrote him up and told him he wasn't allowed on the premises. They sent him a registered letter saying he could not return to the classroom. So, he was arrested when he tried to get into his classroom [. . .] These were fifth graders, ten years old crying and embracing each other because their teacher has been removed from the classroom.

The dismantling of the school was so pervasive that all the new teachers from Laurel Canyon did not get tenure.

> "I was let go. I did not get tenure. The new principal did not sign on my Apple loan. I did not get the loan reduction," said one of the former teachers who left the school after an unsuccessful effort to privatize it.

Teachers at Cabrillo Elementary School and teacher educators at Laurel Canyon were wondering why the assaults against the school were so insidious and destructive:

> *Teacher*: One of the major arguments we would have is that the district was moving toward standards-based instruction and standards-based reporting . . . and our argument was that the way the Learning Record was organized with the scale by grade levels included all of the standards, but it didn't restrict to each grade level. That was a major push for the main part. So we thought that they were looking to mainstream their approach to basic instruction, so the fact that we had all these special programs and we didn't give reporting grades . . .
>
> *Interviewer*: You didn't give report grades?

Teacher: No, it was on merit, based on student's work, on observations, on their portfolios.

Interviewer: No letter grades?

Teacher: No.

Teacher: They were piloting in our school, of all places, they were piloting a new report card that was standard based. So we would show them look, you see the standards there, you see the scales, that's exactly parallel because everything was based on the [California] state standards of education, and we are not inventing things here. We are using resources and frameworks for our correction.

Interviewer: By that time, were they beginning to implement the mandatory testing?

Teacher: Yes. And our parents had high percentage waivers.

Interviewer: Of the test?

Teacher: Yes. Not only did we have waivers for bilingual education, but we also had many parents waiving for standardized testing.

Ramiro, one of the junior teachers at the school, believed the school was a social experiment for the kind of institutionalized control that the standardized movement and No Child Left Behind would develop to take control of public schools.

> So that's how they went after us [. . .] So we are in belief that that was part of the situation. That we were pawns in a larger move. We thought it was based on our use of the Learning Record and our approach to multilinear education, multiage education, we thought it was all of these progressive informed pedagogies that were making us.

Cabrillo Elementary School was an example of teachers' resistance, parents' engagement, and wide-ranging support for authentic assessment, particularly for English-language learners. That was something that could not be tolerated in the face of the homogenization that had taken place to remove the tradition of local control of schools.

The school as it was functioning before—a safe place of learning for working-class, immigrant students who were successfully achieving—was dismantled. In the name of accountability and excellence, Glen and Larry ruined and shattered the dreams of hundreds of bilingual students for whom education was the only possibility for social mobility. Cabrillo Elementary School became one the first casualties when the standardization movement arrived at LCU's College of Education.

SECTION V: THE DISINTEGRATION OF THE TEACHER EDUCATION PROGRAM

Glen's and Larry's areas of influence expanded not only through the newly created PhD in urban leadership, but also their constant presence in the neighboring school districts allowed them to assume the role of power brokers as they marketed themselves as experts in urban education. They used their influence to report back to the College of Education about the alleged disappointment that district officials were expressing concerning the quality of Laurel Canyon teachers. Samantha contended that those allegations were contradicted by rigorous evaluations and feedback from district administrators that were hiring the LCU graduates.

Additional actions by the university leaders added more pressure on teacher education and precipitated a series of unpleasant events. The LCU Office of Development has promised the department of teacher education to match a five-million-dollar, career-ladder grant for bilingual teachers that Beth and Miriam, the associate directors, had obtained. That was one of the conditions the university accepted when the grant was awarded to the university. The grant had funded a very successful program that allowed Laurel Canyon to recruit a very diverse and competitive pool of teachers.

However, in the midst of all the tensions created by Glen and Larry, and the conflict with Miriam, the associate director, Samantha learned that the president of the university refused to provide the matching money for teacher education despite the development office's commitment and request. The president had communicated his decision to Edward, the dean of the college some months earlier, but he never communicated this news to Samantha, despite the fact that this decision could ultimately interrupt the daily operations at the department.

Samantha could not believe that the university president had agreed to the conditions of the grant, had signed the documents, and now, he was refusing to support teacher education. Samantha was shocked. She knew at that moment that they were pushing her out. Without that money she could not effectively run teacher education. Samantha said that at that moment it was obvious to her that the university wanted her out as soon as possible.

Progressively, the teacher education program at Laurel Canyon University began to lose its cohesiveness. It was like a domino effect. One event precipitated other events. Supervisors and teacher education faculty who had always opposed some of the changes that Samantha had implemented in the program found this time a friendly ear in Larry, Glen, and the other White male faculty, Joseph the school psychologist.[1] When Samantha demanded her faculty align their teaching, advising, and supervision to the philosophy of the teacher preparation program, they went to the College of Education to complain about her.

That summer, Miriam resigned. She invited faculty and students of color to a special meeting to explore whether she could obtain a collective resignation to support her claim that she was being harassed. People supported Samantha instead, but the impact of that resignation and Miriam's action were very painful for Samantha.

Days later, a critically distraught Samantha went to the provost office and in tears told her she was resigning immediately as the director of the teacher education department. She said she could not take it anymore. She said she could manage the attacks by Glen and Larry, but she could not bear the accusations presented by Miriam and the way she departed.

She said that her level of despair and hopelessness was overwhelming, and after not being able to sleep or eat for many days she decided it was time for her to leave teacher education. She had led the program for eight years—three years as assistant director and five years as director. Her resignation was immediately accepted, and she was told she could stay at the College as an education faculty but she had to give up teacher education.

> "That was crazy to me. It showed me they didn't understand anything I'd tried to do," said Samantha.

To prove that she was well intentioned, she promised to stay at the university as a faculty during the following fall semester to help with the transition. Her dream to seriously transform the culture of teacher education had been crushed. She did not understand exactly what had happened.

SECTION VI: REPACKING TEACHER PREPARATION INTO A NEW NEOLIBERAL FORMAT

The university called Kristine and urgently asked her to come back and take over teacher education in the fall semester. She did not waste any time. She appointed Glen's protégée as her associate director and kept Beth as the assistant director of the program. Kristine began turning teacher preparation into a highly religious experience. She asked faculty to hold hands and pray at some events. She brought her Bible to the department and asked the students to pray, including during classes. She released one the faculty she considered to be a supporter of Samantha's ideas. Others left before she arrived.

Kristine decided to change the philosophy of the teacher preparation program to focus on "excellence and accountability." Later on, she changed it to "social justice and accountability," conscious of the powerful marketing effect of including the term *social justice* in the program. She encouraged Glen and Larry to teach graduate classes for the teachers, focusing on test scores and standards. Glen took some of the students in his courses to Texas to experience what he considered were *miracle* schools for their work with testing.

The fury of the transition was so traumatic that the student teachers could not understand how suddenly all the gains and insights they had experienced in the program were gone in a matter of months. There was a generalized sense of loss. The students began rebelling. They wrote messages on the listserv complaining about what they felt were the conservative and repressive views of Kristine.

One of the bilingual teachers posted a message on the listserv complaining about the new leadership of the teacher education department. Teresa, who had been following the situation in the background, stepped into the online discussion and wrote a message supporting the student's views about Kristine and expressing her strong disappointment at the newer conservative direction of the program.

What Teresa did not know is that news of that criticism arrived at the College of Education. Kristine, using the email that Teresa had send to the listserv, approached each of the faculty members at the College of Education and demanded an urgent faculty meeting to address the issue. Teresa arrived to the faculty meeting after attending a conference abroad unaware of the conversations that had been happening in her absence.

That is when most of the attacks took place. Teresa was ruthlessly scolded in that meeting. One by one, her colleagues criticized her actions, and she was told that the college was not going to tolerate any more criticism of Kristine and her new policies in teacher education.

> They told me I could no longer be trusted, and accused me of trying to destroy the teacher education program and the College of Education . . . the hazing was so brutal that I could not speak nor find words to respond to their attacks.

The marginalization of Teresa, a senior professor, was so severe that even the staff was afraid to talk to her. People walked by her and ignored her. "She was treated like dust," said Samantha. Teresa decided to leave Laurel Canyon for a year, and she became a visiting professor at another university to see whether things would calm down.

Meanwhile, Samantha was forced to empty her office in the teacher education building to give room to Kristine. The university put all her belongings in a small cubicle in the basement of the College of Education. That was her office while she taught her last course at Laurel Canyon. She was aware she was a non grata person in that institution. By the end of the fall semester she left the university heartbroken and humiliated.

Teresa returned to Laurel Canyon at the end of that academic year, and she realized that her level of ostracism was worse. After writing a letter to her colleagues and her students, she decided to resign her position as a senior, tenured professor at the university. In spite of the indignation of the students and their support, she was forced to quit as Samantha had.

Teresa and Samantha were not friends—on the contrary, they distrusted each other—but they both believed that teacher education had to change to create possibilities for democratic schooling. That vision made them the target of exclusionary practices as the university was unapologetically turning into a corporation of higher education. Teresa and Samantha were ostracized, denigrated, and repudiated as members of the faculty body. Their ideology and theoretical contributions were antithetical to the corporate goals of the university.

Meanwhile, Kristine was very successful in turning the department of teacher preparation into one of the most conservative programs in the university. Her new mantra was "social justice and accountability," and under the social justice name she began glorifying the wonders of standardization and testing as fundamental for the achievement of minority students.

Her hard work paid off when she was appointed dean of the College of Education. The previous dean, Edward, lost his job because he was blamed for not being able to control Samantha's transformational efforts in teacher education. In another ironic twist, Kristine was demoted from her position of dean four years later after the university learned that the friend she had hired as her associate dean and tenured professor at Laurel Canyon was at the same time an active tenured faculty at another university. The university removed Kristine as the dean of the College of Education and fired her friend, but she was allowed to remain on the faculty despite the discovery of her questionable practices.

NOTE

1. Joseph became the new provost of the university the following year after an intense restructuring of the College of Education and the university.

SEVEN

Analyzing the Efforts to Transform the Teacher Education Culture

WHAT COULD SAMANTHA HAVE DONE DIFFERENTLY?

Samantha made the mistake of accepting a tenure-track position that was combined with an administrative position. She was hired as an administrator and as an assistant professor. The two jobs were in opposition to each other. Samantha's major responsibility was to manage teacher education. That position was eminently administrative, but in addition, she was expected to teach, carry out academic research, publish, and perform service as someone who did not have any administrative responsibilities.

One of the serious problems that affected Samantha's decision to transform the program was that she excessively trusted the university. She lost sight that she was a junior professor who in spite of leading the teacher education program for several years was still treated condescendingly by her colleagues. She failed to recognize that she was going to be evaluated for promotion and tenure by senior faculty who had a very different vision of how to run teacher education.

As a junior, untenured faculty, Samantha had not yet created a support system within the College of Education that would have sustained her when her senior colleagues attacked her. She tangentially kept some sort of relationship with Teresa and the other faculty, but she had not developed a strong political alliance with them that would have shielded her from the brutal attacks against her policies.

In addition, Samantha was so overworked and so profoundly immersed in the daily direction of teacher preparation that she did not make any effort to participate or to develop a friendly network of administrators. She lost sight that she needed the unconditional support of the dean of the college, the provost, and the president of the university to implement those important changes in teacher education.

Samantha also felt that she could carry out the transformational efforts at teacher education alone. Teresa's presence in the university through her doctoral students and teacher education faculty may have given Samantha the impression that the time was ripe to implement those changes. After all, Teresa had been very unapologetic about her public stances on issues of democratic schooling and got tenure and promotion successfully.

But what Samantha overlooked is that Teresa's only job during her junior faculty years at the university was to teach and publish prolifically while getting grants to create her own research institute. In addition, during Teresa's early career stages she had developed a great working relationship with the previous provost, which may have protected her from the negative comments and attacks of her colleagues.

Samantha thought she could run teacher education freely as Kristine had done without any problem. While Samantha was an associate director she had relied on Kristine's popularity in the university ranks to run teacher education without any interference. However, when she became the director and she was on her own, she thought she could modify Kristine's policies in teacher education without any problem. She was wrong.

Samantha overlooked the powerful forces of the university and never paid attention to the fact that the College of Education and the university had become major corporate entities in spite of their alleged academic goals. Laurel Canyon had been part of Samantha's life since she got her teaching credential there. She considered Laurel Canyon her academic home and the faculty her family. Samantha failed to consider that institutions do not have personal loyalties, much less corporatized universities that react to the fluctuations of the market once their financial resources are being compromised.

Samantha's biggest problem was her lack of strong management skills. She had been hired to do administration, but she considered herself a scholar overseeing the ideological and intellectual direction of the program. This is why she had hired Beth. However, in her attempts to give faculty and students of color more visibility and power within the department she created another assistant director position for bicultural affairs, at the same rank of Beth but with different compensation and social benefits.

According to Samantha, this inconsistency was caused by the decision of the College of Education to grant Beth all the additional perks she demanded for her return. She said she did not have any other option than to agree to what the university had negotiated with her. That was an administrative disaster that resulted in a major *racialized* conflict during Samantha's tenure. Lost in this racial politics were Samantha's progressive credentials and cultural politics that had made it possible to implement progressive changes at the LCU's teacher preparation program.

Samantha needed a powerful mentor in the college and the university in addition to a strong political network before she embarked in all the changes to contest the culture of teacher education. Her only mentor had been Kristine, and she was not willing to protect someone who had seriously reversed the ideological orientation of teacher preparation at Laurel Canyon.

LESSONS FROM TERESA'S DEPARTURE

Teresa had been a professor at Laurel Canyon for fifteen years when she resigned her tenured position. Like Samantha, she trusted the university administrators and her senior colleagues, and after a long struggle to get tenure she let her guard down. She overlooked the ideological position of the new provost and the corporate turn of the university.

After all, Teresa had been absent for two years after a long sabbatical and Kristine had been in an equally lengthy research leave, so their conflicts had been substantially reduced. However, what happened during those years was that Teresa lost her network of internal supporters and the alliances she had developed before her absence had weakened.

In addition, Teresa had immersed herself into organizing a statewide teacher movement that was supported by Samantha, some of the teacher education faculty, and some doctoral students. The popularity of the movement, and the fact that for the very first time Teresa had real chances of influencing the transformation of teacher education through the changes that Samantha and Miriam were implementing, created a serious concern in the College of Education.

The attacks against Samantha were also directed at Teresa, who, as resilient as she was, did not foresee how convoluted and powerful were the forces that were disarticulating this transformational project. She trusted that the same senior faculty who gave her tenure were going to honor her academic right to disagree in public about the conservative restoration of teacher education. She was also wrong.

The way the college slashed her was as cruel as when they got rid of Samantha. Teresa had more options, probably most of them in court, but she was very tired of fighting to be accepted in a university that since the beginning repudiated her ideological stance. She left without spending much time planning her departure or her future. She was deeply hurt.

The mobbing that had systematically happened at the College of Education (Davenport, Schwartz & Elliott, 1999) had left her traumatized and disoriented. She could not look back because if she saw deeply she would have realized that she never should have accepted a position in that place.

The transformative efforts at Laurel Canyon University would have had greater chances of success if Samantha and Teresa had joined forces, planned their journey together, and had overcome their mutual distrust to become political allies in their quest to transform the culture of teacher education. Together, they would have become powerful players in the larger power arrangement of the college and the university.

Between Teresa's doctoral students and Samantha's teacher interns, they would have had the possibility of shaking the very foundation of Laurel Canyon University. However, they both failed to make strong connections and alliances with top university administrators. Individually, they did not have any independent financial resources that could have been used to level their political and academic standing in the university. They focused so much on the transformational efforts at the college of education and at teacher preparation that they lost sight of the financial role of the institution.

THE SUCCESSES AND CONTRADICTIONS OF THE CHANGES AT LCU'S TEACHER PREPARATION PROGRAM

The changes that Samantha had infused into the teacher education program at Laurel Canyon University were implemented in the context of a very contradictory environment. The department she was leading was situated in one of the most elitist higher-education institutions in the area. Bicultural and working-class students were baffled by their participation in a university that was financially inaccessible to most students from underprivileged backgrounds.

In spite of the aspirations of the leadership of the teacher education department to become a program for social justice, students assumed large student loans that compromised their financial future and the promise of social mobility. The financial cost of teacher preparation is a serious issue for students of color. The cost is so excessive that very often they give up their aspirations to become teachers. However, when these students decide to pursue a teaching credential they understand they will spend most of their active lives paying student loans because teaching is not a profitable career (Claycomb & Hawley, 2000; Miller & Endo, 2005; Nicklos & Brown, 1989; Vanden Brook, 1993).

However, the small-size classes and the individualized attention that the teacher preparation program offered at Laurel Canyon was very effective in helping historically marginalized students get a graduate education and become excellent teachers. This experience was in contrast with what happens at large universities. Researchers (Gossett et al., 1996; Nora & Cabrera, 1996) have confirmed that minority students in large, predominantly white universities feel isolated: "The potential for alienation and isolation from majority students is evident, ultimately resulting in a potentially negative impact on self concept and confidence" (Nichols, 2006, p. 128).

The three-tier support system offered by the teacher education department at Laurel Canyon (cohort model, small teacher-student ratio, and small advisory group) helped student teachers endure the intensity of the program. It also provided them with a safe space to process new visions of teaching and learning that very often contradicted their own schooling experience.

The success of the cohort model has been extensively documented both as a fundamental factor to retain students of color into teacher education and also as a major element to progressively transform teacher preparation (Bennett, 2002; Carter, 2006; Irizarry, 2007; Villegas & Davis, 2007; Waddell & Ukpokodu, 2012).

Samantha's leadership was fundamental to making changes to the philosophy of the program and to move teacher education from a traditional multicultural department to an intended program for social justice. The transition from a policy of "colored bodies" to an antiracist/antibiased pedagogy was possible because of Samantha's political commitment.

She deliberately recruited faculty who had been trained in critical educational thought, many of whom were Teresa's former students. In fact, in one of her famous lectures Teresa said, "Institutions can change because they are governed by people who can infuse their own political and philosophical values in the direction of their programs."

Similar research (Fitts & Weisman, 2010; Moody, 2004) also suggests that when there is political intention and a thoughtful commitment, the composition of the faculty and student body can be altered by deliberately recruiting nontraditional students and teacher educators. As Ukpokodu (2007) asserts,

> A reconceptualized teacher education will recognize the importance and value of faculty/student diversity and so will strive to create a balance in the faculty/student composition. Bold efforts must be embarked upon to recruit as well as retain faculty/students of color who are currently underrepresented in teacher education programs. (p. 12)

In addition, there is a need to create safe spaces for underrepresented students and faculty (Ukpokodu, 2007; Waddell & Ukpokodu, 2012), and a support system in the form of mentorship, academic assistance, fellowships, and financial aid to support that effort. Samantha, Miriam, and Beth were very successful at writing and obtaining large grants to support the recruitment and retention of students of color. One of the most successful grants geared toward diversifying the student body was the career ladder grant for bilingual educators. Another grant was obtained to prepare math and science teachers from monolingual and bilingual backgrounds.

The reorganization of the teacher education curriculum was vital to infuse the program with a unified vision of its philosophy of teaching. The efforts to connect the method courses to the theoretical and philosophical classes created a more integrated vision of its social justice orientation. The changes in the curriculum would not have worked without bringing more faculty and instructors that were representative of the students and the ideas that the program was trying to sponsor.

This ethnography suggests that in spite of the control of state agencies, teacher education programs have freedom to implement some changes or to use the current impositions of standardized tests to improve their own curriculum. That was the case with the literacy classes at Laurel Canyon when one of the most hated state exams became vital to target and improve the literacy courses in the program while offering teachers the opportunity to learn emancipatory visions of literacy.

The examination of traditional teaching practices at all the levels of the program—introductory courses, student-teaching experience, teacher action research projects, and the entire curriculum—demonstrated that social justice needed to be related to the daily practices of teachers.

Because the reproduction of social inequalities is subtly carried in the implementation of those detrimental but naturalized pedagogical practices, the program pointed out how teachers were innocently playing the role of ideologues of the system and offered alternative roles for them.

The success of the teachers at Laurel Canyon resided on the fact that they were prepared to face the uncertain realities of public schools. During their teacher preparation, student teachers were able to move beyond a missionary approach to understand the conservative and contradictory nature of schools. The program made teachers aware that they were going to teach in working-class communities and that their students were going to be second-language learners and students from nonmainstream backgrounds with different academic levels and learning experiences.

Student teachers spent their first year of training in culturally diverse schools and continuously discussed their daily experiences and reactions to that reality in the context of their courses at the program. The permanent reflection of the teachers at Laurel Canyon was manifested in the daily and weekly journals that they kept during their entire teacher education program. At every monthly meeting, faculty supervisors analyzed their teachers' journals along with their colleagues to provide a more responsive and coherent support system for the students' teaching experience.

The Action Research Project was one of the most complex assignments and was considered the catalyst that created a holistic transformation of the teachers' lives. It was through that project that the teachers at Laurel Canyon realized the complexity of their role and the limitations of their previous beliefs about teaching.

In sum, the changes at Laurel Canyon University suggest that the efforts to break the hegemonic cycle of reproduction of inequalities in teacher education are more feasible than expected. However, taking into account the reproductive nature of teacher education, its role as one of the ideological state apparatuses, and the corporatization of higher education, these changes should have been conducted with caution and preceded by a series of strategic steps to secure the feasibility of that transformational effort.

REFLECTIONS ON THE APPROPRIATION OF MULTICULTURALISM AND SOCIAL JUSTICE IN TEACHER EDUCATION

What became clear in this ethnography is that the "multicultural" orientation of the College of Education was a discursive practice that was never intended to be interpreted genuinely. The talk and alleged commitment to diversity of the university and the college of education were marketing discourses that made faculty—including Samantha, Teresa, and the students—believe they could create structural change.

Severe problems arise when faculty and students of color are brought to academic institutions with the assumption that their departments and classrooms are safe places when "democratic dialogue [is] possible and happening did not make it so" (Ellsworth, 1994, p. 314). It does not matter how much a teacher preparation department is labeled multicultural or a social justice program if "the culture of power that exists in the classroom involves conditions of structural oppression" (Applebaum, 2009, p. 387). As Applebaum (2009) asserts, "When certain voices do not want to engage in such critical reflection and are given the floor to express their views, the marginalized are injured again" (p. 400).

The teacher preparation program at Laurel Canyon was not aware of the complexities of bringing such a large group of minority students and faculty into the college of education. However, because of the high number of people from underrepresented backgrounds and the theoretical preparation that Teresa had instilled in them, there was an important mass of critical people that secured a tenuous space. As Ramiro, one of the bilingual teachers, remembers,

> I think in many respects it was a fast track program so there was always a large turnover of students and so there was always camaraderie with people who were in the field, out on the field, researchers. So the cycle was completed there, and it was a safe space for having these conversations. The content, of course, considering the complete dismantling of valuable education here in [California], and still that a school would have liked that kind of students having those critical conversations was important . . . that you have a place to have those conversations. Even about race, they're having conversations, critical

conversations about race and what does it mean in our society as educators. So, where the vast majority of people felt comfortable talking
about race. Here was a space where you were gonna [*sic*] be pushed to
consider our analysis of where we exist.

In spite of that fact that the teacher education program at Laurel Canyon provided a small space for growth and important dialogues, one of
the most important lessons of this experience is to understand that the
struggle for social justice needs to be visualized as a very serious and
complex journey. The marketable trend to appropriate the concept of
social justice trivializes the seriousness of such efforts, and it reduces this
constant and fluid process to a static and consummated state, as if the
label is enough to create a conversion in the program and to reorganize
the social structures where power is maintained and reproduced.

Because power never gives up by itself, any significant change will
happen only at the price of serious, organized strategic efforts. Therefore,
it is essential to analyze the sincerity of such engagement and the powerful impact that these particular decisions have on students and faculty.

CAN THE CULTURE OF TEACHER EDUCATION REALLY BE TRANSFORMED?

Samantha's and Teresa's stories are not unique in teacher education, particularly in contexts like this where the transformational efforts appear to
be more authentic. Yet does this mean that teacher education programs
cannot be changed? Is an authentic vision of social justice incompatible
with the reproductive nature of teacher education? Is social justice in
contradiction with the financial principles of corporatized universities
that rely exclusively on teacher education as the major source of income?

Since the beginning of the twentieth century when schools became
mass-culture institutions, they assumed a powerful role in shaping social
consciousness. In fact, Althusser identified schools as one of the leading
ideological apparatuses. Schools play an authoritative role in reproducing society's ideology, and they have innocently disguised domination
under the form of instructional discourses and pedagogical practices (Giroux, 1980).

But schools are not the only places implicated in the hegemonic process of reproduction. Teacher training programs have also played a vital
function in shaping America's ideology. Teacher education programs
have become the quintessential ideological apparatuses in securing the
transmission of the values of the dominant society. This is why they are
tightly controlled through accreditation and other scheming mechanisms.

Teacher preparation programs represent one of the most efficient institutions to assure that the common citizen will agree with the hegemonic forces and ideologies that keep them oppressed. Teacher education will

procure that consent through the teachers they are preparing and through the discourses and instructional practices their teachers will implement in their classrooms. It is in schools where the forces of the market are able to create consumer identities and naturalize the rampant inequalities of capitalism.

However, the research at Laurel Canyon University uncovers that the procurement of consent that is instilled into the preparation of teachers is not perfect, but on the contrary, there is a permanent resistance to that hegemonic discourse, and both forces coexist as part of the dialectical process of teacher preparation. Yet what this case study uncovers is that the political power and transformative potential of teacher education may even be greater than its reproductive nature, but only if this resistance is articulated, institutionalized, and strategically put into practice.

This ethnography suggests that in spite of the control of state agencies and the bureaucratic restrictions that teacher preparation programs face on a daily basis, there are possibilities of articulating an emancipatory discourse and implementing strategies to educate teachers for social action. Samantha was able to galvanize a variety of individual efforts to create institutional changes.

Encouraged by the theoretical and ideological training of many of her teacher education faculty, Samantha steadily began articulating a vision to transform teacher preparation. Samantha was very clear that the social changes the student teachers wanted to see in society had to be initiated in teacher education. She faced structural obstacles and contradictions along the way, but she was a visionary, for she was able to identify the areas of teacher preparation that needed a major transformation.

EIGHT

Reflections and Implications of This Study for Teacher Education

THE MISAPPROPRIATION OF DIVERSITY AND SOCIAL JUSTICE

There are many teacher preparation programs in the United States that have incorporated the term *social justice* into their names, mission statements, conceptual frameworks, or visions of teacher preparation. Many of them were encouraged by the promise of national accreditation, more political visibility, and higher enrollment. Several of these programs and their leaders share a superficial vision of cultural diversity represented mostly in a policy of colored bodies and in a celebration of food, heroes, and festivals.

The ethnography at Laurel Canyon University reveals that this was the motivation behind the "multiculturalism" of the university and its teacher education program. What these programs and their leaders did not foresee was the implication of bringing a critical mass of colored bodies into their once homogeneous college of education, who were able to develop critical consciousness to question and to confront the practices and structures that kept them excluded. This was what precipitated the dismantling of the transformational efforts of this teacher preparation program.

The co-option of cultural diversity and social justice characterized by the continuous recruitment of students of color who are not given any power in the decision-making process of the university or teacher preparation is an aberration to Dewey's (1916) vision of schools as "little democracies." Yet what it is more discouraging is that this co-option of the revolutionary struggles of past generations has been naturalized by neoliberalism and its intention to replace public education with corporate models of schooling.

The newer CAEP national accreditation standards are a manifestation of this appropriation of social justice and cultural diversity. By 2016, teacher education programs will be accredited nationally only when they prove with hard data that their teachers are "diverse" and "excellent" as demonstrated by their performance in the top third of the GRE, ACT, or SAT scores. This is the same discourse that Kristine, the director of the teacher education department at Laurel Canyon University, implemented after the previous transformational changes at teacher education were crashed. Her new mantra was "excellence and accountability" and later, "social justice and accountability."

In this kind of teacher education program, student teachers lose their cultural identity to conform to the hegemonic values of hard-work ethic and excellence. Their success proves that there is no structural constrains to achieve "excellence" but just the commitment to work hard. At the end, through an intensive schooling in this culture, they become convinced that the dominant interpretation of their success is legitimate. They embrace the ideology of the dominant society. They become assimilated.

That is exactly what neoliberalism as a form of governmentality is about. Individuals become rational subjects whose goal in life is to be self-sufficient. They blame themselves for their own failures regardless of the structural constraints they may face. "A 'mismanaged life' becomes a new mode of depoliticizing social and economic powers and at the same time reduces political citizenship to an unprecedented degree of passivity and political complacency" (Brown, 2003, p. 15).

These are the teachers that NCATE and now CAEP seek to train. They will be the new, diverse teaching force of the twenty-first century under the ideology of neoliberalism. They are going to be the fresh, diverse faces of the teaching force with no voice, no consciousness, and no critical awareness.

That is what appears on the horizon of convoluted educational reforms under neoliberalism. However, there are some teacher preparation programs that are authentically seeking to engage their teachers into a critical cultural politics that envision teacher education as the laboratory to form the engaged, critical citizenry that Dewey foresaw at the beginning of the last century.

For those authentic teacher preparations for social justice, this ethnography reveals that there are a series of efforts that need to be implemented to secure the success of such changes. One of the immediate goals is to form the kind of historical blocks and/or historical alliances necessary to assure the success of any transformational effort. They also need to reflect and act upon the following questions: How can new teachers survive in a culture of assessment based on students' test scores while teaching problem-posing pedagogy? How can critical teachers thrive in an environment that uses value-added assessment to evaluate their performance in their job?

How can teacher education programs be enriched by policies that promote a higher number of diverse students while granting them power in the decision-making process? How do they ensure that students' dignity and humanity are going to be not only respected but also become naturally integrated into the voices and discourses of the teacher preparation program? How does the program help diverse novice teachers to deal with the debilitating forces of neoliberal reform and the bashing of public school teachers?

These are the challenges that those genuine transformational efforts face. On top of that, how are those programs dealing with the pressure to shorten and simplify their teacher education program? What kind of teacher education curriculum have they implemented? What are the learning theories and discourses in this teacher preparation program?

More importantly, how are teacher education programs in general able to function in a time of teacher bashing? How can they infuse in their teacher the calling, vocation, and passion for teaching when an entire culture has been developed to criticize, condemn, and degrade public school teachers? These are the challenges confronting teacher education now. This book seeks to provide enough insights to understand the dialectical and difficult task of education for the best citizens that this society can have: the committed teachers who aspire to educate the critical citizenry that Dewey dreamed of forming. This is something that cannot be given up.

IMMEDIATE RADICAL TACTICS, SHORT-TERM RADICAL APPROACHES, AND LONG-TERM STRATEGIES

Paula Allman (1994) discusses how Paulo Freire was successful in launching a radical pedagogical movement based on his pedagogy of the oppressed. She also points out that people are attracted to Freire's philosophy of teaching but complain that he does not provide a clear framework to carry out emancipatory, radical projects. However, Allman argues that people have misread Freire because they are not familiar with the philosophical and ideological roots of critical theory that were developed in the neo-Marxist tradition of the first part of the twentieth century in Europe.

Allman contends that a clear analysis of Freire's writings reveals they are full of strategies to engage in what she calls "immediate radical tactics, [and] short-term radical approaches, [which are] critically conceived and practiced within or integral to the long-term strategy" (Allman, 1994, p. 1). However, Allman as well as Freire caution that the call for articulating and implementing radical tactics, approaches, and strategies as part of a radical praxis does not require the formulation of a checklist or steps to carry out "revolutionary social transformation," for every single situation must respond to its historical and political context.

Nevertheless, the ethnography at Laurel Canyon University suggests that there may be a series of "tactical struggles" with "radical potential" that critical educators for social justice may engage not only to transform the culture of teacher education but also to avoid being pushed out of their academic and administrative positions within the university. This book provides some recommendations to transform the culture of teacher education as part of a larger project to democratize public schooling.

RECOMMENDATIONS FOR FACULTY

What follows is a series of suggestions to engage in small tactic struggles and larger political and academic changes in teacher education.

Faculty engaged in transformational efforts in teacher education should develop strong alliances (Gramsci, 1971)—political blocks—with other faculty in their departments, schools, and colleges, and the larger university, who can support them through their political project.

These alliances should transcend racial, linguistic, ethnic, religious, gender, sexual, or physical differences. These coalitions should extend to all the levels of seniority in the department and should continue to the top ranks of the university administration. Strategic alliances with top university administrators are fundamental for the uninterrupted success of any effort to transform the culture of teacher education.

Faculty should encourage the formation of student organizations and should support any student effort to institutionalize their participation in the direction of the teacher education program. Students are a fundamental component of the life of the university, and faculty engaged in transformational efforts should focus their energy on creating safe spaces and forums where students develop their organizational skills and political voice.

Activist faculty in teacher education programs should develop immediate radical tactics and short-term radical approaches only if they are part of their larger transformational efforts. They should fight only those battles that are clearly related to the final goals in order to remain credible and emotionally strong.

Faculty activists who play administrative roles should be cautious about the possible contradictions of these positions with their academic jobs. They should become knowledgeable about how the university evaluates faculty and whether their administrative contribution is explicitly included as part of the faculty evaluation. Administrative positions are more difficult to be managed by untenured, junior faculty, as any changes they may carry out will be used against them once they are evaluated for promotion and tenure.

In addition, administration entails a series of very organized efforts that need to be aligned to the culture of the larger university. Faculty needs to make sure they are not inheriting dysfunctional work relationships or positions that may later backfire at them. They also need to make sure they have enough administrative support to handle their administrative positions.

Junior faculty should make an effort to become less vulnerable to attacks by senior faculty. They may need to be stronger scholarly, demonstrate a superior teaching performance, and volunteer within rational limits to serve the university and larger professional organizations.

Activist faculty should make an effort to bring their own financial resources to the university in the form of grants, fellowships, or other income to support their own political projects, and to create enough economic leverage to compensate for any attack or assault against their efforts.

Junior faculty should seek the protection of a mentor who not only introduces them to the culture of the department and the university but also protects them when conflicts escalate.

Finally, faculty must take care of their own well-being. They should develop a clear cultural politics that can allow them to discern whether the university where they work is clearly supporting their academic and political efforts. Faculty should not have to give up their personal life, health, and financial stability to remain employed at a higher education institution. Those may be early signs that a faculty is not adequately supported by the department and the larger university.

RECOMMENDATIONS TO REEXAMINE THE CULTURE OF TEACHER PREPARATION

What follows is a series of recommendations that are inspired in Teresa's teaching and Samantha's transformational effort at the Laurel Canyon teacher education program. Samantha and Teresa insisted that any change in the larger society needed to be initiated in teacher education. They argued that the most concrete ways to create a connection between school and the larger diverse society was to reconceptualize the entire curriculum and the administrative practices of teacher education.

A teacher education program committed to prepare teachers for social justice and cultural democracy should make an attempt to examine the following components of its teacher preparation:

Banking Education and the Production of Docile Citizens

Teacher education should critique and examine the implications of using a banking approach to teach culturally diverse and working-class students. Teacher education should encourage teachers to form critical students rather than submissive individuals.

Teacher education should encourage teachers to democratize their classrooms by discussing and negotiating with their students the class rules. Teacher education should question traditional detrimental pedagogical practices and authoritarian disciplinary models that keep culturally diverse students dropping out of schools. It should question the system of rewards and punishment that is so pervasive in the school system, and it should analyze its implication for culturally diverse students.

Particularly, teacher education should question grouping by ability label and tracking practices that keep masses of working-class students in low-paid jobs. Teacher education should encourage creative ways to implement cooperative learning strategies in heterogeneous groups.

Curriculum and the Integration of Subjugated Knowledges

Teacher education should advocate a student-responsive curriculum. It should advocate multiple literacies as a way of "reading the world" rather than only "reading the word." It should advocate a whole-language approach in literacy with a balanced and strong integration of phonics in meaningful contexts.

Teacher education should emphasize a problem-posing pedagogy over a problem-solving approach. It should advocate the design of curricula that clearly integrates students' experiences, culture, and knowledge as vital components. It should question prepackaged curricula because they assume that teachers are managers of classrooms rather than cultural workers.

Teacher education should question the official knowledge (curriculum) and should deconstruct the unproblematic glorification of technology and positivism at schools. It should deconstruct the neutrality of certain subjects like math, algebra, and science and should advocate student-need-based strategies to teach these subjects.

Teacher education should present teachers different paradigms that explain the learning process, but it should encourage teachers to move beyond developmental and behaviorist approaches as they tend to "psychologize" teaching and learning.

Teacher education should expose the real nature of testing and meritocracy. It should encourage teachers to use inclusive and democratic methods of assessment. It should examine the political, economic, and pedagogical dimensions of homework and grading policies.

Schools Are Mirrors of the Larger Society

Teacher education should ask teachers to conduct research in the communities in which they work. It should ask teachers to learn about the lives of their students and families.

Teacher education should ask teachers to define and reflect on their socialization process and their impact on their teaching. It should ask teachers to reflect on their stereotypical assumptions and how they define their students' expectations and performance.

Teacher education should ask teachers to examine society's power structure and identify their own social and political location as well as their students. It should ask teachers to be conscientious about the dangers of cultural tokenism, and encourage them to practice an authentic cultural democracy.

Teacher education should emphasize that an education for cultural democracy cannot be confined to the addition of a couple of courses dealing with multiculturalism, but rather, that the issue of cultural diversity and social justice must be embedded into the entire teacher education curriculum. Teacher education should encourage teachers to become advocates of active bilingualism, multilingualism, and biculturalism.

Teacher education should become aware that through its curriculum, fieldwork placement, discoursive practices, and pedagogical experiences student teachers could either become ideological agents of the dominant society or advocates for social change.

The reproduction of social inequalities is not a perfect or static cycle. There are always possibilities to articulate a resistance to the use of teacher education as the most powerful ideological apparatus.

References

Adams, M., Bell, L. A. & Griffin, P. (Eds.). (2007). *Teaching for diversity and social justice.* New York: Routledge.

Allman, P. (1994). Paulo Freire's contributions to radical adult education. *Studies in the Education of Adults, 26* (2), 1–17.

Althusser, L. (1969). *For Marx.* New York: Vintage Books.

Althusser, L. (1971). Ideology and the ideological state apparatuses. In B. Brewster (Trans.), *Lenin and philosophy and other essays.* New York: Monthly Review.

Amrein, A. L. & Berliner, D. C. (2003). The effects of high-stakes testing on student motivation and learning. *Educational Leadership, 60* (5), 32–38.

Anderson, G. (1989). Critical ethnography in education: Origins, current status, and new directions. *Review of Educational Research, 59* (3), 249–70.

Anyon, J. (1980). Social class and the hidden curriculum of work. *Journal of Education , 162,* 67–92.

Anyon, J. (1981). Social class and school knowledge. *Curriculum Inquiry,* 11 (1), 3–42.

Apple, M. W. (1978). The new sociology of education: Analyzing cultural and economic reproduction. *Harvard Educational Review, 48* (4), 495–503.

Apple, M. W. (1979). *Ideology and curriculum.* London and Boston: Routledge & Kegan Paul.

Apple, M. W. (1982). *Education and power.* Boston: Routledge & Kegan Paul.

Apple, M. W. (1993). *Official knowledge: Democratic education in a conservative age.* New York: Routledge.

Apple, M. W. & King, N. (1977). What do schools teach? In R. H. Weller (Ed.), *Humanistic education.* Berkeley: McCutchan.

Apple, M. W. & Weis, L. (1983). *Ideology and practice in schooling.* Philadelphia: Temple University Press.

Applebaum, B. (2009). Is teaching for social justice a "liberal bias"? *Teachers College Record, 11* (2), 376–408.

Arato, A. & Gebhardt, E. (Eds.) (1978). *The essential Frankfurt School reader.* New York: Urizen Books.

Aronowitz, S. (1981). Preface to the Morningside Edition. In P. Willis, *Learning to labor: How working class kids get working class jobs* (ix–xiii). New York: Columbia University Press.

Ayers, W., Hunt, J. A. & Quinn, T. (Eds.) (1998). *Teaching for social justice: A democracy and education reader.* New York: New Press, Teachers College Press.

Baltodano, M. (2006). The accreditation of schools of education and the appropriation of diversity. *Cultural Studies-Critical Methodologies Journal, 6* (1), 123–42.

Baltodano, M. & Clemons, A. (2005). Appropriating the discourse of diversity: Trends in the accreditation of teacher education. *International Journal of Diversity in Organizations, Communities and Nations, 4,* 309–17.

Bennett, C. (2002). Enhancing ethnic diversity at a Big Ten university through project TEAM: A case study in teacher education. *Educational Researcher, 31* (2), 21–29.

Berliner, D. C. & Biddle, B. J. (1995). *The manufactured crisis: Myths, fraud, and the attack on America's public schools.* New York: Addison Wesley Longman.

Bernstein, B. B. (1971–1975). *Class, codes, and control.* London: Routledge & Kegan Paul.

Bernstein, B. B. (1977). *Class, codes, and control: Towards a theory of educational transmissions* (2nd ed.). London: Routledge & Kegan Paul.

Beyer, L. E. (1989). Reconceptualizing teacher preparation: Institutions and ideologies. *Journal of Teacher Education, 40,* 22–26.

Beyer, L. E. & Zeichner, K. (1987). Teacher education in cultural context: Beyond reproduction. In T. S. Popkewitz (Ed.), *Critical studies in teacher education.* Philadelphia: Falmer Press.

Bourdieu, P. (1977). Cultural reproduction and social reproduction. In J. Karabel and A. H. Halsey, *Power and ideology in education* (487–510). New York, Oxford: Oxford University Press.

Bourdieu, P. & Passeron, J. C. (1977). *Reproduction in education, society, and culture.* Beverly Hills, CA: Sage.

Bowles, S. & Gintis, H. (1976). *Schooling in capitalist America.* New York: Basic Books.

Bullough, R. V., Jr. (2014). Toward reconstructing the narrative of teacher education: A rhetorical analysis of preparing teachers. *Journal of Teacher Education, 65* (3). DOI: 10.1177/0022487113519131.

Carnegie Forum on Education and the Economy. Task Force on Teaching as a Profession. (1986). *A nation prepared: Teachers for the 21st century. The report of the task force on teaching as a profession.* New York: Carnegie Forum on Education and the Economy.

Carspecken, P. F. (1996). *Critical ethnography in educational research.* New York: Routledge.

Carspecken, P. & Apple, M. (1992). Critical qualitative research: Theory, methodology, and practice. In M. D. LeCompte, W. L. Millroy, and J. Preissle (Eds.), *The handbook of qualitative research in education* (507–51). San Diego, CA: Academic Press.

Carter, D. (2006). Key issues in the persistence of underrepresented minority students. *New Directions for Institutional Research, 130,* 33–46.

Clandinin, D. J. et al. (Ed.). (1993). *Learning to teach, teaching to learn: Stories of collaboration in teacher education.* New York: Teachers College Press.

Claycomb, C. & Hawley, W. D. (2000). *Recruiting and retaining effective teachers for urban schools: Developing a strategic plan for action.* College Park, MD: University of Maryland. Retrieved from http://files.eric.ed.gov/fulltext/ED451147.pdf.

Cochran-Smith, M. & Fries, M. K. (2001). Sticks, stones, and ideology: The discourse of reform in teacher education. *Educational Researcher, 30* (8), 3–15.

Cochran-Smith, M. & Lytle, S. L. (Eds.) (1993). *Inside/outside: Teacher research and knowledge.* New York: Teachers College.

Conquergood, D. (1991). Rethinking ethnography: Towards a critical cultural politics. *Communication Monographs, 58* (2), 179–94.

Council for the Accreditation of Educator Preparation. (2013). *CAEP Accreditation Standards.* CAEP Board of Directors. Retrieved from http://caepnet.org/standards/standards/.

Darder, A. (1991). *Culture and power in the classroom.* New York: Bergin & Garvey.

Darling-Hammond, L. (1985). *Data on teachers and teaching: Opening the black boxes of education.* Washington, DC: National Center for Education Statistics.

Darling-Hammond, L. (1998). *Doing what matters most: Investing in quality teaching.* California Education Policy Seminar and the California State University Institute for Educational Reform. Sacramento, CA: CSU Institute for Educational Reform.

Darling-Hammond, L. (2000). Teacher quality and student achievement: A review of state policy evidence. *Education Policy Analysis Archives, 8* (1).

Darling-Hammond, L. (2001). *The research and rhetoric on teacher certification: A response to "teacher certification reconsidered."* National Commission on Teaching and America's Future. Stanford University, Palo Alto, CA.

Darling-Hammond, L. (2006). Constructing 21st-century teacher education. *Journal of Teacher Education, 57* (3), 300–14.

Darling-Hammond, L., Wise, A. E. & Klein, S. P. (1995). *A license to teach: Building a profession for 21st-century schools.* Boulder, CO: Westview.

Davenport, N., Schwartz, R. D. & Elliott, G. P. (1999). *Mobbing: Emotional abuse in the American workplace.* Collins, IA: Civil Society Publishing.

Derrida, J. (1977). *Of grammatology*. G. C. Spivak (Trans.). Baltimore: Johns Hopkins University Press.

Dewey, J. (1916). *Democracy and education*. New York: MacMillan.

Diesing, P. (1971). *Patterns of discovery in the social sciences*. New York: Aldine.

Doyle, W. (1996). Themes in teacher education research. In J. Sikula (Ed.), *Handbook of research on teacher education* (3–24). New York: MacMillan.

Du Bois, W. E. B. (1935). Does the Negro need separate schools? *Journal of Negro Education, 4* (3), 328–35.

Ellsworth, E. (1994). Why doesn't this feel empowering? Working through the repressive myths of critical pedagogy. In L. Stone (Ed.), *The education feminist reader* (300–27). New York, Routledge.

Fitts, S. & Weisman, E. (2010). Exploring questions of social justice in bilingual/bicultural teacher education: Towards a parity of participation. *Urban Review, 42*, 73–393.

Foucault, M. (1977). *Discipline and punish: The birth of the prison*. New York: Pantheon.

Foucault, M. (1980). *Power/knowledge: Selected interviews and other writings*. C. Gordon (Trans.). New York: Pantheon Books.

Frank, C. (1999). *Ethnographic eyes: A teacher's guide to classroom observation* . Portsmouth, NH: Heinemann.

Freire, P. (1970). *Pedagogy of the oppressed*. New York: Seabury Press.

Freire, P. (1994). *Pedagogy of the oppressed*. New York: Continuum.

Gabbard, D. A. (1999). *Knowledge and power in the global economy: Politics and the rhetoric of school reform*. New York: Routledge.

Giroux, H. A. (1980). Teacher education and the ideology of social control. *Journal of Education, 162*, 5–27.

Giroux, H. A. (1981). *Ideology, culture, and the process of schooling*. Philadelphia: Temple University Press.

Giroux, H. A. (1983). *Theory and resistance in education*. New York: Bergin & Garvey.

Giroux, H. A. (1988). *Teachers as intellectuals: Towards a critical pedagogy of learning*. New York: Bergin & Garvey.

Giroux, H. A. (2004). Cultural studies, public pedagogy, and the responsibility of intellectuals. *Communication and Critical/Cultural Studies , 1* (1), 59–79. http://dx.doi. org/10.1080/1479142042000180926.

Giroux, H. A. (2008). *Against the terror of neoliberalism: Politics beyond the age of greed*. Boulder, CO: Paradigm.

Giroux, H. A. & McLaren, P. (1987). Teacher education as a counter public sphere: Notes towards a redefinition. In T. S. Popkewitz (Ed.), *Critical studies in teacher education* (266–97). Philadelphia: The Falmer Press.

Giroux, H. A. & McLaren, P. (1988). Teacher education and the politics of democratic reform. In H. A. Giroux (Ed.), *Teachers as intellectuals* (158–85). Boston: Begin & Garvey.

Giroux, H. A. & Pena, A. N. (1979). Social education in the classroom: The dynamics of the hidden curriculum. *Theory and Research in Social Education, 7* (1), 21–42.

Giroux, H. A. & Purpel, D. (1983). *The hidden curriculum and moral education: Deception or discovery?* Berkeley: McCutchan.

Gossett, B., Cuyjet, M. & Cockriel, I. (1996). African Americans' and non-African Americans' sense of mattering and marginality at public, predominantly white institutions. *Equity and Excellence in Education, 29* (3), 37–42.

Graham, P. A. (2003). Foreword. In D. T. Gordon. *A nation reformed? American education 20 years after* A Nation at Risk. Harvard Education Press.

Gramsci, A. (1971). *Selections from prison notebooks*. Q. Hoare and G. Smith (Ed. and Trans.). New York: International Publishers.

Greene, M. (1978). *Landscapes of learning*. New York Teachers College.

Greene, M. (1982). Public education and the public space. *Educational Researcher, 11* (4), 4–9.

Greene, M. (1984). A philosophic look at "merit" and "mastery" in teaching. In G. A. Griffin (Ed.), *The master teacher concept: Five perspectives*. Austin, TX: Research and Development Center for Teacher Education.

Haberman, M. (1988). *Preparing teachers for urban schools*. Bloomington, IN: Phi Delta Kappa Educational Foundation.

Haberman, M. (1995). *Star teachers of children in poverty*. West Lafayette, IN: Kappa Delta Pi.

Hall, S. & Gieben, B. (1992). *Formations of modernity*. Cambridge, UK: The Open University.

Haney, W. (2000). The Myth of the Texas Miracle in education. *Education Policy Analysis Archives*, [S.l.], (8) 41. ISSN 1068-2341. Available at http://epaa.asu.edu/ojs/article/view/432. Accessed August 9, 2014. doi:http://dx.doi.org/10.14507/epaa.v8n41.2000

Harding, S. (1987). Introduction: Is there a feminist method? In S. Harding (Ed.), *Feminism and methodology* (1–14). Bloomington & Indianapolis: Indiana University Press.

Hawkins, B. D. (2013, June 20). *Diverse: Issues in higher education*, 14–15. www.diverseeducation.com.

Held, D. (1980). *Introduction to critical theory*. Berkeley and Los Angeles: University of California Press.

Holmes Group. (1986). *Tomorrow's teachers. A report of the Holmes Group*. East Lansing, MI.

Horton, M. (1998). *The long haul: An autobiography*. New York: Teachers College Press.

Irizarry, J. (2007). "Home growing" teachers of color: Lessons learned from a town-gown partnership. *Teacher Education Quarterly, 34* (4), 87–102.

Jarvie, J. (2014, September 7). School cheating trial set to open. *Los Angeles Times*, A8.

Kincheloe, J. & McLaren, P. (1994). Rethinking critical theory and qualitative research. In N. Denzin & Y. Lincoln (Eds.), *Handbook of qualitative research* . Beverly Hills: Sage.

Kincheloe, J., Steinberg, S. & Villaverde, L. (1999). *Rethinking intelligence: Confronting psychological assumptions about teaching and learning* . New York: Routledge.

Kirk, D. (1986). Beyond the limits of theoretical discourse in teacher education: Towards a critical pedagogy. *Teaching and Teacher Education, 2* (2), 155–67.

Kumashiro, K. K. (2010). Seeing the bigger picture: Troubling movements to end teacher education. *Journal of Teacher Education 6* (1, 2), 56–65.

Laclau, E. (1979). *Politics and ideology in Marxist theory: Capitalism, fascism, populism*. London: Verso.

Lather, P. (1986). Research as praxis. *Harvard Educational Review, 56* (3).

Levinson, B. (1992). Critical ethnography of education. *International Journal of Qualitative Studies in Education, 5*, 205–25.

Levinson, B., Foley, D. E. and Holland, D. (Eds.) (1996). *The cultural production of the educated person: Critical ethnographies of schooling and local practice*. Albany, NY: State University of New York Press.

Lincoln, Y. S. & Guba, E. G. (1985). But is it rigorous? Trustworthiness and authenticity in naturalistic evaluation. In D. Williams (Ed.), *Naturalistic evaluation*. San Francisco: Jossey-Bass.

Liston, D. P. & Zeichner, K. M. (1987). Critical pedagogy and teacher education. *Journal of Education, 169* (3), 117–37.

Macedo, D. (1994). *Literacies of power: What Americans are not allowed to know*. Boulder: Westview.

Marcuse, H. (1960). *Reason and revolution: Hegel and the rise of social theory*. Boston: Beacon Press.

McLaren, P. (1993). *Schooling as a ritual performance* (2nd ed.). New York: Routledge.

McLaren, P. (1994). *Life in schools: An introduction to critical pedagogy in the foundations of education* (2nd ed.). New York: Longman.

McLaren, P. (2002). *Educating for social justice and liberation.* Retrieved from https://zcomm.org/znetarticle/educating-for-social-justice-and-liberation-by-peter-mclaren/.

McLaren, P. & Baltodano, M. (2005). The future of teacher education and the politics of resistance. In P. McLaren et al., *Red seminars: Radical excursions into educational theory, cultural politics, and pedagogy* (131–46). New York: Hampton Press.

McLaren, P. L. & Giarelli, J. M. (Eds.). (1995). *Critical theory and educational research.* Albany, NY: State University of New York Press.

Miller, P. C. & Endo, H. (2005). Journey to becoming a teacher. *Multicultural Education, 13* (1), 2–9.

Moody, J. (2004). *Faculty diversity: Problems and solutions.* New York: Routledge.

Morrow, R. A. & Torres, C. A. (1995). *Social theory and education: A critique of theories of social and cultural reproduction.* New York: SUNY.

National Commission on Excellence in Education. (1983). *A nation at risk: The imperative for educational reform.* Washington, DC: U.S. Department of Education.

National Council for Accreditation of Teacher Education. (2008). *Professional standards for the accreditation of schools, colleges, and departments of education.* National Council for Accreditation of Teacher Education, Washington, DC.

National Council on Teacher Quality. (2013). Teacher prep review 2013 report. Washington, DC. Retrieved from www.nctq.org.

National Governors' Association. (1991). *Time for results: The governors' 1991 report on education.* Washington, DC.

Nichols, J. D. (2006). Project TEAM: First-year analysis at a regional campus site. *The Teacher Educator, 42* (2), 122–39.

Nicklos, L. B. & Brown, W. S. (1989). Recruiting minorities into the teaching profession: An educational imperative. *Educational Horizons, 67* (4), 145–49.

Nora, A. & Cabrera, A. (1996). The role and perceptions of prejudice and discrimination on the adjustment of minority students to college. *Journal of Higher Education, 67* (2), 119–48.

Novak, J. M. (Ed.). (1994). *Democratic teacher education: Programs, processes, problems, and prospects.* New York: SUNY.

Nussbaum, M. (2001). The enduring significance of John Rawls. *The Chronicle of Higher Education.*

Nussbaum, M. (2006). *Frontiers of justice: Disability, nationality and species membership.* Cambridge: Harvard University Press.

Nussbaum, M. C. (2010). *Not for profit: Why democracy needs the humanities.* Princeton, NJ: Princeton University Press.

Payne, R. K. (2003). *A framework for understanding poverty* (3rd ed.). Highlands, TX: Aha! Process.

Popkewitz, T. (1979). *Teacher education as socialization: Ideology or social mission.* Paper presented at the American Educational Research Association Annual Meeting in San Francisco.

Popkewitz, T. S. (1984). *Paradigm and ideology in educational research: The social functions of the intellectual.* London, New York: Falmer Press.

Popkewitz, T. S. (Ed.). (1987). *Critical studies in teacher education: Its folklore, theory, and practice.* London, New York: Falmer Press.

Popkewitz, T. S. (1991). *A political sociology of educational reform: Power/knowledge in teaching, teacher education, and research.* New York: Teachers College Press.

Popkewitz, T. S. (Ed.) (1993). *Changing patterns of power: Social regulation and teacher education reform.* Albany: State University of New York Press.

Popkewitz, T. S. (1997). *Critical studies in teacher education: Its folklore, theory and practice.* Philadelphia: The Falmer Press.

Quantz, R. (1992). On critical ethnography (with some postmodern considerations). In M. D. LeCompte, W. L. Millroy, and J. Preissle (Eds.), *The handbook of qualitative research in education* (447–505). San Diego, CA: Academic Press.

Ravitch, D. (2010). *The death and life of the great American school system: How testing and choice are undermining education.* Philadelphia, PA: Basic Books.

Ravitch, D. (2013). *Reign of error: The hoax of the privatization movement and the danger to America's public schools.* New York: Alfred A. Knopf.

Roman, L. G. (1992). The political significance of other ways of narrating ethnography: A feminist materialist approach. In M. D. LeCompte, W. L. Millroy, and J. Preissle (Eds.), *The handbook of qualitative research in education* (555–94). London: Academic Press.

Roman, L. & Apple, M. (1990). Is naturalism a move away from positivism? Materialist and feminist approaches to subjectivity in ethnographic research. In E. W. Eisner & A. Peshkin (Eds.), *Qualitative inquiry in education: The continuing debate* (38–73). New York: Teachers College Press.

Saltman, K. J. (2009). The rise of venture philanthropy and the ongoing neoliberal assault on public education: The case of Eli and Edythe Broad Foundation. *Workplace, 16,* 53–72.

Sawchuk, S. (2013). Teacher-prep accreditor adopts outcomes standards. *Education Week* (September 2013), 6. www.edweek.org.

Scott, J. (2009). The politics of venture philanthropy in charter school policy and advocacy. *Educational Policy, 23,* 106–36.

Sharp, R. & Green, A. (1975). *Education and social control.* London: Routledge & Kegan Paul.

Shor, I. (1986). Equality is excellence: Transforming teacher education and the learning process. *Harvard Educational Review, 56,* 406–26.

Shor, I. (1992). *Empowering education: Critical teaching for social change.* Chicago: University of Chicago Press.

Simon, R. I. & Dippo, D. (1986). On critical ethnographic work. *Anthropology and Education Quarterly, 17,* 195–202.

Spindler, G. (1988). *Doing the ethnography of schooling* (2nd ed.). Illinois: Waveland Press.

Steinberg, S. & Kincheloe, J. (1998). *Unauthorized methods: Strategies for critical teaching.* New York: Routledge.

Symcox, L. (2009). From *A Nation at Risk* to No Child Left Behind: 25 years of neoliberal reform in education. In J. Andrzejewski, M. Baltodano and L. Symcox (Eds.), *Social justice, peace and environmental education: Transformative standards.* New York: Routledge.

Tanner, D. (1993). A nation "truly" at risk. *Phi Delta Kappa, 75* (4), 288–97.

Tesch, R. (1990). Types of qualitative analysis. In R. Tesch (Ed.), *Qualitative research: Analysis types and software tools* (77–102). New York: Falmer Press.

Thomas, J. (1993). *Doing critical ethnography.* Newbury Park, London: Sage Publications.

Ukpokodu, O. N. (2007). Preparing socially conscious teachers: A social justice–oriented teacher education. *Multicultural Education, 15* (1), 8–15.

United States Department of Education. (1985). *Goals 2000: A progress report.*

Vanden Brook, T. (1993). UWM, UW struggle to keep minorities. *Milwaukee Journal,* 25, B3.

Villegas, A. & Davis, D. (2007). Approaches to diversifying the teaching force: Attending to issues of recruitment, preparation, and retention. *Teacher Education Quarterly, 34* (4), 137–47.

Waddell, J. & Ukpokodu, O. N. (2012). Recruiting & preparing diverse urban teachers: One urban-focused teacher education program breaks new ground. *Multicultural Education, 20* (1), 15–22.

Weiner, L. (1993). *Preparing teachers for urban schools: Lessons from thirty years of school reform.* New York: Teachers College.

Weiner, L. (2007). A lethal threat to U.S. teacher education. *Journal of Teacher Education, 58* (4), 274–86.

Wexler, P. (1987). *Social analysis of education.* London and New York: Routledge & Kegan Paul.

Willis, P. (1977). *Learning to labour: How working class kids get working class jobs.* Farnborough, England: Saxon House.

Willis, P. (1981). *Learning to labor: How working class kids get working class jobs* (2nd ed.). New York: Columbia University Press.

Wolff, R. D. (2005). Ideological State apparatuses, consumerism, and U.S. capitalism: Lessons from the left. *Rethinking Marxism, 17* (2), 223–35.

Zeichner, K. M. (2006). Reflections of a university-based teacher educator on the future of college- and university-based teacher education. *Journal of Teacher Education, 57* (3), 326–40.

About the Author

Marta P. Baltodano is a professor in the Department of Specialized Programs in Urban Education at Loyola Marymount University. Her research focuses on the corporatization of schools of education, teachers' beliefs on social justice, and interracial conflicts in Los Angeles. Her teaching includes issues of critical educational theory, political economy, globalization, social justice, and qualitative methodologies. Baltodano is the president-elect of the Council of Anthropology and Education (CAE) of the American Anthropological Association, and contributing editor of CAE for *Anthropology News*, and cochair of CAE's Mission Committee. She is one of the founding members of the California Consortium for Critical Educators (CCCE) and the founder of the American Educational Research Association's (AERA) special interest group Critical Educators for Social Justice (CESJ). She was the 2008 to 2009 program cochair of AERA's Division G (Social Context of Education). Baltodano coedited the book *The Critical Pedagogy Reader"* (Darder, Baltodano & Torres, 2002, 2008) and the compendium *Social Justice, Peace and Environmental Education: Transformative Standards* (Andrzejewski, Baltodano & Symcox, 2009). She is the author of the book *The Appropriation of Social Justice in Education* (in press), and she has published several articles in peer-refereed journals and is currently writing a book about the corporatization of education.